Digitalization and Competition Policy in Japan

Shuya Hayashi · Koki Arai

Digitalization and Competition Policy in Japan

Springer

Shuya Hayashi
Graduate School of Law
Nagoya University
Nagoya, Aichi, Japan

Koki Arai
Faculty of Business Studies
Kyoritsu Women's University
Chiyoda City, Tokyo, Japan

ISBN 978-981-99-5309-7 ISBN 978-981-99-5310-3 (eBook)
https://doi.org/10.1007/978-981-99-5310-3

This Springer imprint is published by the registered company Springer Nature Singapore Pte Ltd.
The registered company address is: 152 Beach Road, #21-01/04 Gateway East, Singapore 189721, Singapore

Paper in this product is recyclable.

Preface

This book summarizes the development of new competition law in this era of digitalization, focusing on the framework and cases in Japan. Although the focus is on Japan, Japanese competition law today has much in common with the rest of the world, and faces common challenges in responding to the digital age.

Competition law is a method of government intervention in the marketplace. The recent development of digitalization has drastically changed the market. Therefore, competition law also needs to respond to this change. This is a phenomenon occurring not only in Japan but around the world.

Digitalization can be organized into five categories from the perspective of cost reductions attributable to digital technology: (a) lower search costs, (b) lower reproduction costs, (c) lower transportation costs, (d) lower tracking costs, and (e) lower verification costs (Goldfarb and Tucker, 2019). One could also model digitalization as a revenue shifter and identify conditions under which digitalization is pro-competitive or anti-competitive (De Cornière and Taylor, 2021). In addition, when modeling digitalization, one could organize from cases where firms obtain data without strategic interaction, where firms collect data from interactions with consumers, and where firms obtain data from data intermediaries (Pino, 2022). Alternatively, we can focus on the characteristics of information products and their sale, and the interaction between firms and data intermediaries, distinguishing between pre-sales of information (the buyer acquires the information structure) and post-sales (the buyer pays for a concrete realization) (Bergemann and Bonatti, 2019). The analysis of digitalization has itself been approached in different ways.

Competition laws, although with country-specific differences, are designed to prohibit actions that restrict competition and attempt to achieve free competition in the market. However, today, there is a growing body of case law that provides some guidelines.

This book introduces these guidelines in the form of explanations of cutting-edge research papers and is intended not to be a specific casebook, but rather to bridge the boundary between research and practice.

Based on these aims, this book is structured as follows.

Chapter 1 is an overview of competition law. It is based on Arai (2021) but is newly structured by referring to the system of antitrust law and recent cases in Europe, the US, and Japan and carefully explaining the issues in those cases.

Chapter 2 is the international cooperation in competition law, which is based on International Cooperation and Harmonization in Competition Law "Zeitschrift für Japanisches Recht 1 (Journal of Japanese Law) 24(47) 133–144, May 2019," but the overall structure of the chapter has been significantly revised to incorporate the latest information. It carefully explains the need for international cooperation, noting that Europe, the USA, and Japan have many characteristics in common in their competition laws.

After the intro part, the second part of the book describes the digital approach of Japanese competition law.

Chapter 3 explains the development of competition law under the development of big data and AI. On competition policy and the development of big data and artificial intelligence, using "The Roles of Innovation in Competition Law Analysis 162–177 (ii) December 2018" as a basis for this chapter, with subsequent developments and a review from the perspective of the chapter's structure are discussed. In addition, it develops a discussion of how to cut through big data and AI.

Chapter 4 places particular emphasis on the perspective of what competition law should do with big data and AI. "How Competition Law Should React in the Age of Big Data and Artificial Intelligence, The Antitrust Bulletin, 64(3), 447–456, 2019." is used as a basis for this chapter but with an emphasis on the specific issues that competition law should address.

Chapter 5, based on the paper "A Methodology for Assessing High-Tech Regulation: A Legitimacy Perspective," published in the International Review of Law, Computers & Technology, 35(3), 288–300, 2021, organizes perspectives on high-tech regulation. It examines the direction of thinking related to regulation itself, including the perspectives required by the legitimacy approach and the sufficiency perspective in the context of digitalization.

The third part then summarizes the realities of various digital regulations. This part examines, in particular, various regulations, various empirical analyses, etc., from the viewpoint of how to grasp the social facts, as opposed to actual real-world phenomena.

Chapter 6 is on data regulation. It is based on the paper "International Rules for Online Platform Operators: Focusing on the Debate over the Transfer and Distribution of Data," Yearbook of International Economic Law, (29), 75–98, 2020. In addition to this, the chapter also examines the legal system that regulates data and how it should be established internationally.

Chapter 7 is about digital platform regulation. It is based on the paper, "Aspects of International Rule-Making Concerning Digital Platforms: The So-Called 'One Country, Two Systems' Issue and Legal Disciplines Concerning Data Transfer and Distribution," which is addressed to the Nextcom: Prospects for the Present and Future of Information and Communications, 41(41), 4–13, 2020. Digital platform regulation is progressing in Europe, the USA, and Japan. This chapter is a multifaceted study of measures to deal with this situation, based on a fundamental perspective of competition in the marketplace.

Chapter 8 is an empirical analysis of the reality of competition in multifaceted markets that is based on "Business Diversification and Multifaceted Markets." International Journal of Economic Policy Studies, 2021. As an actual example of multifaceted markets, the empirical analysis is explained using Japanese private railway companies as a case study. Although the chapter is based on a research paper, we believe that one of the tasks of this book is to introduce the way this initiative was conducted as a way of recognizing the current state of the digital market.

Chapter 9 is Competition Law and Consumers on Digital Platforms. "Digital Platform and Consumer Rights—From the Perspectives of Competition Law and 'Trust'" (Shuya Hayashi and Koki Arai) ASCOLA 2021. This is a new drawing based on ASCOLA 2021. Until now, market regulation has focused mainly on how to deal with suppliers. This chapter presents the results of a new study that explores how to regulate the market from a new perspective, i.e., that of the consumer, and how to regulate the market in a necessary and sufficient manner.

Chapter 10 is based on a chapter in "Issues and Theories of Contemporary Economic Law (Collection of Essays in Honor of Professor Takatsugu Kanai)" titled "Recent Issues Concerning Licensing of Standard Essential Patents: Focusing on the European Debate." The paper is based on a chapter in the book "Issues and Theories of Modern Economic Law (Essays in Honor of Professor Takatsugu Kanai's 70th Birthday)" and is supplemented by an overview of recent major contentious cases in Europe and their issues, as well as some discussion of the issues.

Chapter 11 is concerned with the realization of a digital society and the regulation of law, particularly from the perspective of new technologies and the future of law, and considers the challenges and risks associated with the digitalization of society, as well as the state of law in a digital society. It is basically a newly written manuscript, although the original manuscript of a dialogue in a law-related journal was used as a reference.

In the final chapter, we briefly conclude what we believe to be the current state of competition law in the midst of digitalization, which we have examined in this book, and summarize its limitations and challenges.

We hope that readers who have studied the basics of Japanese competition law will regard this book as a further intermediate or advanced reference and as an indication of the current position of how researchers think about the issues to be addressed in the future. At the same time, the authors will be very pleased if the book is widely read not only by researchers but also by practitioners and people in other fields. We hope this book will further stimulate their interest in competition law, competition policy, and empirical industrial organization theory in the progress of digitalization.

We would like to express our gratitude to Yutaka Hirachi and Rajasekar Ganesan, the editors of this book, for their great assistance and patience. We are very grateful to Yuichiro Hayakawa, Megumi Tahira, Sei Shishido, Yoshitaka Tsuruta, and Kentaro Hirayama for their comments and participation in the discussion in the very early versions of the papers on which the chapters of this book are based. We are also thankful to Kunlin Wu for his help in reviewing and proofreading this book.

This research project was supported by JSPS Grant-in-Aid for Scientific Research (19K01610 and 23K01404) and RISTEX JPMJRX21J1. The book is the partial result of the joint research project with KDDI Research, Inc., Japan, and partly owes its inspiration to Shuya Hayashi's recent research stay in Germany as a visiting scholar (Max-Planck-Institut für ausländisches und internationales Privatrecht (April 2022–March 2023) and Institut für Handels- und Wirtschaftsrecht, Universität Bonn (October 2022–March 2023)). We would like to express gratitude to three anonymous referees for their comments.

Nagoya, Japan — Shuya Hayashi
Chiyoda City, Japan — Koki Arai

References

Arai (2021) Data distribution and competition law issues: proceedings of 2021 International Conference of Big Data, IEEE Xplore. https://doi.org/10.1109/BigData52589.2021.9671329. 2021

Bergemann and Bonatti (2019) Markets for information: an introduction, Annual Review of Economics, 11:85–107 (Volume publication date August 2019) https://doi.org/10.1146/annurev-economics-080315-015439

De Cornière A, Taylor G (2021) Data and competition: a simple framework, with applications to mergers and market structure. Toulouse School of Economics Working Papers 1076. https://drive.google.com/file/d/1WFVUqYecWTkestv_RHJDbNPH8ygBPQ4M/view

Flavio Pino (2022) The microeconomics of data—a survey. J Ind Bus Econ

Goldfarb A, Tucker C (2019) Digital economics. J Econ Lit, 57(1):3–43. https://doi.org/10.1257/jel.20171452

List of First Publications (Mainly in Japanese)

Chapter 1:
Original.

Chapter 2:
Shuya Hayashi, International Cooperation and Harmonization in Competition Law in Zeitschrift für Japanisches Recht (Journal of Japanese Law) 24(47) pp. 133–141 (2019).

Chapter 3:
Koki Arai, Big Data and AI, Competition policy and the development of big data and artificial intelligence in The Roles of Innovation in Competition Law Analysis pp. 162–177 (2018).

Chapter 4:
Koki Arai and Shuya Hayashi, How Competition Law Should React in the Age of Big Data and Artificial Intelligence. In The Antitrust Bulletin 64(3) pp. 447–456 (2019).

Chapter 5:
Koki Arai and Shuya Hayashi, A Methodology for Assessing High-Tech Regulation: A Legitimacy Perspective. In International Review of Law, Computers & Technology, 35(3) pp. 1–13 (2021).

Chapter 6:
Shuya Hayashi, International Discipline on Online Platform Operators: Focusing on the Debate over Data Transfer and Distribution in Annual Review of the Japan Association of International Economic Law (29) pp. 75–98 (2020).

Chapter 7:
Shuya Hayashi, Aspects of International Rule Formation for Digital Platformers: The So-Called "One Country, Two Systems" Issue and Legal Discipline on Data Transfer and Distribution in Nextcom 41(41) pp. 4–13 (2020).

Chapter 8:
Koki Arai and Shuya Hayashi, Business Diversification and Multifaceted Markets in International Journal of Economic Policy 15(2) pp. 235–255 (2021).

Chapter 9:
Shuya Hayashi and Koki Arai, Digital Platform and Consumer Rights—From the Perspectives of Competition Law and "Trust"in ASCOLA 2021 presentation.

Chapter 10:
Shuya Hayashi, Recent Issues Concerning Licensing of Standard Essential Patents in Theories and Challenges of Contemporary Economic Law, pp. 375–392 (Kobundo Publishing 2022).

Chapter 11:
Original.

Contents

Part I
Introduction

Part I provides an overview of competition law in Japan, the US, and the EU and the state of international cooperation in the field of competition law, which plays an important role in the effective functioning of economic mechanisms in the liberal economy.

Chapter 1
Overview of Competition Law

1 Concept of Competition Law

The real-world laws discipline the relationships of human life and are used as standards for establishing and judging rights relationships between individuals. When considering the prohibition of cartels, typically, the Japanese Antimonopoly Act regulates cartels as an unreasonable restraint of trade. The U.S. antitrust laws and European competition law also provide similar provisions.

Thus, if law is one of the tools of social discipline, economics can provide theoretical support for such laws and analyze their evaluation measures and actual effects. To do so, economics uses models that abstract from reality, examines the implications of those models, and conducts econometric analysis using actual statistics and aggregate data.

For example, in economics, the idea that competition is desirable is based on the following. The first theorem of welfare economics states that perfectly competitive markets lead to a Pareto efficient allocation of resources. This is achieved when demand is adjusted so that the marginal rate of substitution equals the price ratio on the demand side and production is adjusted so that the marginal rate of conversion equals the price ratio on the supply side. As a result, the benefits of exchange are realized, supply at minimum cost through efficient allocation of labor, and optimal production levels for each good. This perfectly competitive equilibrium maximizes social surplus, which is the sum of producer surplus and consumer surplus. However, when there is only one firm in the market, its control over prices and quantities may reduce social surplus to a level below that of perfect competition.

Legal thinking in these various situations is based on statutory concepts to determine social facts. In typical legal thinking, a required fact must exist according to legal requirements, and the burden of proof is placed on the claimant of this required fact. Failure to meet this burden of proof renders the claim inadmissible. However, there are also crimes and defenses (re-defenses), which will be determined by the court when the case is ripe for trial. Other policy responses, such as the Biden Presidential Decree, are also being considered.

S. Hayashi and K. Arai, *Digitalization and Competition Policy in Japan*,
https://doi.org/10.1007/978-981-99-5310-3_1

2 Competition Law Provisions

The provisions of competition laws in Japan and the U.S. and EU are generally similar. The two main pillars of competition law in these countries are the regulation of collusion, such as cartels, as an act that restricts competition, and the regulation of monopolistic acts that abuse market dominance to prevent the functioning of the competition mechanism. In addition to these, the laws impose ex ante restrictions on mergers to prevent the formation of firms that would dominate the market through business combinations. In Japan, in addition to these regulations, there is a special provision prohibiting the abuse of a superior bargaining position, and this provision is actively applied in the digital sector to tackle the imbalance of bargaining power between parties to a transaction.

Particularly, in the digital context, which is the subject of this book, all of these laws and regulations may apply and have been enforced in practice (see Sect. 3 for details).

2.1 Japanese Antimonopoly Act

The Japanese Antimonopoly Act (Act on Prohibition of Private Monopolization and Maintenance of Fair Trade (1947, Law No. 54)) sets forth the basic rules to be followed by businesses and others in conducting business activities in a liberal economy. In order to promote free and fair competition, the Antimonopoly Act prohibits businesses from hindering free competition or using unfair means of competition. It provides:

Article 3 of the Antimonopoly Act states

An enterprise must not effect private monopolization or unreasonable restraint of trade.

In this regard, Article 2, Paragraph 5 of the Antimonopoly Act states that the legal term "private monopolization" used in this Act means such business activities, by which any enterprise, individually or by combination, in conspiracy with other enterprises, or by any other manner, excludes or controls the business activities of other enterprises, thereby causing, contrary to the public interest, a substantial restraint of competition in any particular field of trade.

Article 2, paragraph 6 defines the term "unreasonable restraint of trade" as business activities, by which any enterprise, by contract, agreement or any other means irrespective of its name, in concert with other enterprises, mutually restrict or conduct their business activities in such a manner as to fix, maintain or increase prices, or to limit production, technology, products, facilities or counterparties, thereby causing, contrary to the public interest, a substantial restraint of competition in any particular field of trade.

2.2 U.S. Antitrust Laws

U.S. competition law, also known as antitrust law, consists of the Sherman Act (1890), the Clayton Act (1914), and the Federal Trade Commission (FTC) Act (1914). The core of the Sherman Act (15 USC §1–7) consists of Section 1 (prohibition of restraint of trade) and Section 2 (prohibition of monopolies).

Section 1 of the Sherman Act states that "Every contract, combination in the form of trust or otherwise, or conspiracy, in restraint of trade or commerce among the several States, or with foreign nations, is declared to be illegal. Every person who shall make any contract or engage in any combination or conspiracy hereby declared to be illegal shall be deemed guilty of a felony, and, on conviction thereof, shall be punished by fine not exceeding $100,000,000 if a corporation, or, if any other person, $1,000,000, or by imprisonment not exceeding 10 years, or by both said punishments, in the discretion of the court." This includes not only cartels between competing companies (horizontally restricting acts) but also acts between companies at different stages of a transaction (vertically restricting acts). This Article applies to joint acts by multiple entities and not to single acts.

Section 2 provides that "Every person who shall monopolize or attempt to monopolize, or combine or conspire with any other person or persons, to monopolize any part of the trade or commerce among the several States, or with foreign nations, shall be deemed guilty of a felony, and, on conviction thereof, shall be punished by fine not exceeding $100,000,000 if a corporation, or, if any other person, $1,000,000, or by imprisonment not exceeding 10 years, or by both said punishments, in the discretion of the court." Both single acts and joint acts are subject to the application of this provision.

2.3 EU Competition Law

In the EU, the European Commission, together with national competition authorities, directly enforces EU competition rules in Articles 101–106 of the Treaty on the Functioning of the European Union (TFEU), which aims to make the EU market work better by ensuring that all companies compete equally and fairly on their own merits.

Article 101 of the TFEU states,

> 1. The following shall be prohibited as incompatible with the internal market: all agreements between undertakings, decisions by associations of undertakings and concerted practices which may affect trade between Member States and which have as their object or effect the prevention, restriction or distortion of competition within the internal market, and in particular those which:
>
> (a) directly or indirectly fix purchase or selling prices or any other trading conditions;
>
> (b) limit or control production, markets, technical development, or investment;
>
> (c) share markets or sources of supply

(d) apply dissimilar conditions to equivalent transactions with other trading parties, thereby placing them at a competitive disadvantage

(e) make the conclusion of contracts subject to acceptance by the other parties of supplementary obligations which, by their nature or according to commercial usage, have no connection with the subject of such contracts.

2. Any agreements or decisions prohibited pursuant to this Article shall be automatically void.

3. The provisions of paragraph 1 may, however, be declared inapplicable in the case of:

- Any agreement or category of agreements between undertakings,

- any decision or category of decisions by associations of undertakings,

- any concerted practice or category of concerted practices,

which contributes to improving the production or distribution of goods or to promoting technical or economic progress, while allowing consumers a fair share of the resulting benefit, and which does not

(a) impose on the undertakings concerned restrictions which are not indispensable to the attainment of these objectives;

(b) afford such undertakings the possibility of eliminating competition in respect of a substantial part of the products in question.

Article 102 of the TFEU states,

1. Any abuse by one or more undertakings of a dominant position within the internal market or in a substantial part of it shall be prohibited as incompatible Such abuse may, in particular, consist of the abuse of the internal market.

2. Such abuse may, in particular, consist in:

(a) directly or indirectly imposing unfair purchase or selling prices or other unfair trading conditions;

(b) limiting production, markets or technical development to the prejudice of consumers;

(c) applying dissimilar conditions to equivalent transactions with other trading parties, thereby placing them at a competitive disadvantage.

(d) making the conclusion of contracts subject to acceptance by the other parties of supplementary obligations which, by their nature or according to commercial usage, have no connection with the subject of such contracts.

Among these provisions, those frequently discussed in the digital context are private monopolization, monopolization, and abuse of a dominant position as standalone acts.

2.4 Business Combination Regulations

There are also regulations on business combinations in the competition laws of various countries. They all prohibit business combinations that would substantially restrict competition. Generally, companies notify the competition authorities before merger, and the merger is only approved after a merger review by the competition authorities. Competition authorities will enjoin business combinations that would restrict competition.

In recent years, killer acquisition, in which promising startups are merged with competitors before they have even been introduced to the market, has become a particular problem.

2.5 Enforcement Agencies

The U.S. has the Antitrust Division of the Department of Justice and the Federal Trade Commission, while the EU has the European Commission in charge of enforcing competition rules and within the Commission the Directorate-General for Competition (DG COMP) is responsible for enforcement. In Japan, the Japan Fair Trade Commission (JFTC) exists and the General Secretariat of the JFTC is in charge of law enforcement.

3 Enforcement of Competition Law in the Digital Sector

Below are several examples of competition law enforcement in the digital sector in Japan, the EU and the US. In particular, it can be seen that the authorities in each country have been aggressively enforcing the law against BigTech in recent years.

3.1 Japan

3.1.1 Case Against Amazon Japan, LLC

The company was found to have engaged in acts such as reducing the amount stipulated in an inventory compensation agreement from the amount of payment due to the supplier in question, who was suspected of being inferior to the company in terms of bargaining position.

In September 2020, the JFTC notified Amazon Japan of the commitment procedures and received an application for approval of the commitment plan from Amazon Japan. The implementation of the plan resulted in the restoration of the monetary value of approximately 2 billion yen in total to approximately 1400 of the suppliers in question.

3.1.2 Case Against Apple Inc.

In the operation of the App Store for iPhone applications, based on the App Store Review Guidelines, Apple Inc. required developers to use a billing method (IAP) designated by Apple when selling digital content within their applications. The company has been implementing these measures.

In September 2021, when the JFTC pointed out the above-mentioned problem to Apple, Apple proposed to allow out-links (including buttons or external links in apps that lead consumers to purchase digital content purchased from websites, etc.) for reader apps (apps used exclusively for viewing digital content purchased from websites, etc.) and to revise the App Store Review Guidelines.

3.1.3 Case Against Rakuten Group, Inc.

In “Rakuten Ichiba”, when the total amount of one order is 3980 yen or more, the “shipping charge” will not be added to the selling price of the product. In March 2020, the JFTC issued an emergency injunction (which was withdrawn due to Rakuten Group’s action). Later, in December 2021, the JFTC issued an injunction against Rakuten Group, Inc., and pointed out this problem, which was reported that Rakuten Group had taken remedial measures. It was announced that the examination would be completed after confirming that the company had implemented the remedial measures.

3.2 U.S.

Recently, U.S. antitrust enforcement actions against platform giants such as Google and Facebook have been underway. On October 20, 2020, the U.S. Department of Justice (DOJ) and 11 other states filed suit against Google in the U.S. District Court for the District of Columbia for alleged violations of Section 2 of the Sherman Act. On December 9, 2020, the FTC filed a lawsuit against Facebook for alleged violations of Section 5(a) of the FTC Act based on violations of Section 2 of the Sherman Act, which was dismissed in June 2021 but re-filed in August. In addition, on December 16, 2020, nine states, including Texas, filed a lawsuit against Google for alleged violations of Section 2 of the Sherman Act, among others, and on December 17, 2020, 37 states, including Colorado, filed a lawsuit against Google for alleged violations of Section 2 of the Sherman Act.

3.2.1 DOJ Lawsuit Against Google

The DOJ’s complaint against Google is comprised of eight sections: (1) nature of the lawsuit, (2) jurisdiction, (3) industry background, (4) relevant market, (5) anticompetitive conduct, (6) anticompetitive effects, (7) alleged violation, and (8) request for relief. In brief, DOJ’s complaint consists of three parts: the first seeks an injunction against Google’s monopolization (i.e., the intentional creation or maintenance of monopoly power) of general search services. The second claim is an injunction against Google's monopoly of search advertising, and the third claim is an injunction against Google's monopoly of general search text advertising.

3.2.2 FTC's Complaint Against Facebook

The FTC alleges that Facebook has monopolized personal social networking in the U.S. Facebook's anticompetitive conduct consists of three main parts. First, its acquisition of Instagram and its continued dominance in the personal social networking. Second, the acquisition and continued control of Whatsapp eliminated a significant threat to Facebook's monopoly competition in personal social networking, and third, the acquisition and continued control of Instagram eliminated a significant threat to Facebook's monopoly competition in personal social networking. Additionally, anti-competitive conditions have been established and enforced regarding access to the API platform that can be used to develop apps for Facebook in order to reduce the competitive threat to the social network monopoly.

The amended complaint also alleges that Facebook launched the Facebook platform as an open space for third-party software developers and then abruptly changed course, requiring developers to agree to terms that would prevent successful applications from posing a competitive threat to Facebook. It alleges that it required developers to agree to terms and conditions. As a result, consumers were deprived of a promising and disruptive heretic. Moreover, the amended complaint presents new direct evidence that Facebook has a dominant share of the U.S. personal social networking market and the power to eliminate competition by putting actual and potential competitors out of business.

3.3 EU and UK

3.3.1 Review Launched for Alleged Anti-competitive Conduct by Google and Meta in Online Display Advertising

In March 2022, the European Commission opened a formal examination of an agreement between Google and Meta regarding online display advertising services for alleged violations of EU competition law.

Google, through its "Open Bidding Program" and other programs, provides an advertising technology service that mediates between advertisers and publishers (media companies) by bidding for online display ad spaces on websites and mobile apps in real time. Meta provides online display advertising services and participates through its "Meta Audience Network" in bidding for third-party publisher ad spaces using Google's and competitors' ad technology services.

The subject of the Commission's review is the September 2018 agreement between Google and Meta to allow Meta's Audience Network to participate in Google's Open Bidding program (codenamed "Jedi Blue" within Google). The Commission finds that the Agreement is not a violation of Google's obligations under the Open Bidding Program. The Commission is concerned that the Agreement is an effort to exclude advertising technology services that compete with Google's Open Bidding program, which may limit or distort competition in the online display advertising market to the detriment of publishers and ultimately consumers.

If such facts are established, the conduct under review may violate EU competition law (Article 101 [Restrictive Competition Agreements] and/or Article 102 [Abuse of a dominant market position] of the Treaty on the Functioning of the European Union).

The Commission will conduct a detailed examination of the case as a matter of priority. The commencement of the formal examination does not prejudge its outcome.

In addition, the UK Competition and Markets Authority ("CMA") has also commenced its own investigation into the agreement between Google and Meta. The Commission is in regular contact with the CMA and will cooperate closely with the CMA on this investigation in accordance with the applicable rules and procedures.

3.3.2 Notice of Objections Sent to Apple

In May 2022, the European Commission (the "Commission") notified Apple of its preliminary finding that it was abusing its dominant position in the mobile wallet market on iOS devices. Apple restricts competition in the market for mobile wallets on iOS devices by restricting access to standard technologies (Near-Field Communication (NFC) or tap and go) used for contactless payments by mobile terminals in stores.

The Commission is concerned that Apple is preventing mobile wallet app developers from accessing the necessary hardware and software (NFC input) on Apple terminals in order to take advantage of its own payment solution, Apple Pay.

3.4 Enforcement Points in the Digital Sector

There are three challenges to promoting competition in the digital sector: first, to determine whether the current digital sector is at a certain stage of growth and whether it needs corresponding technical assistance and more development; second, the design of metadata and other schemas and the increasingly development of data exchange and transactions. The formation of markets that move away from relative transactions and the need for platform services are also discussed. Third is the discussion of the economic value generated by the digital platform itself, including the value of data. These challenges are urgent due to the fact that giant platforms are already dominating the market of actual data-based economic activities.

The relationship between, for example, data distribution and competition law in such a digital field is also a subject of research and on the agenda of the Japan Association of Economic Law. Specifically, the following studies have been conducted: a study of digital platforms and the regulation of competitor exclusionary acts with respect to search engines (Takeda 2021), a study of the significance of digital platform regulation in the regulation of abuse of a superior bargaining position, which is a regulation unique to Japan (Shibata 2021), a study of the regulation of business combinations of digital platforms (Wakui 2021) and the effectiveness of problem-solving measures and commitment measures in digital platform cases (Vande Walle 2021), a study on the economic theory of regulation of MFN clauses (Matsushima 2021), and so on. These are the current studies on digital regulation from the perspective of economic law and industrial organization theory. Based on these previous studies, this chapter briefly introduces the case in the United States and focuses on five issues that may arise, especially from the perspective of the development of data distribution markets.

4 Competition Law Issues in Digital Markets

Recent developments in Japan, the U.S., and the EU regarding competition law in the digital field can be summarized as the following issues. Based on the reality of these discussions, let us summarize the important issues for future discussions, including the Japanese cases and the Google and Facebook lawsuits in the U.S. In light of the constitutive requirements of private monopolization as an independent act (Japan), Article 2 of the Sherman Act (US), and abuse of dominant position (EU), we believe the following five are the key issues in these cases. First, the identification of the relevant market. Second, the existence of monopoly power. Third, the act of forming, maintaining, or strengthening market dominance. Fourth, it is necessary to consider whether consumers have been substantially harmed. Fifth, the implementation of measures to resolve the problem, and remedies. These issues should be kept in mind when considering the decision criteria for individual lawsuits and the future relationship between the digital market and competition law.

4.1 Delineation of the Relevant Market

The first is the delineation of the "relevant market," which appears to be the greatest barrier to competition analysis. In enforcing the law, it is important to ensure consistency between the social facts and the language of the law (constitutive requirements). Competition law usually defines a market in terms of a specific field of trade (Japanese Antimonopoly Act) or a relevant market (U.S. Antitrust Law), and then addresses the issue of whether monopoly power exists in that market.

The datasets addressed in the U.S. Google case include local domain websites with search results optimized based on the location of users in the U.S. for targeted marketing by advertisers, as well as targeted messages. The Facebook lawsuit also involves the distribution and monetization of data in the form of selling advertisements that are displayed to users based on personal data about their lives collected by Facebook. In DOJ v. Google, the relevant markets were search services, search advertising, and general search text advertising; in FTC v. Facebook, the relevant markets were personalized social networking.

Typically, the definition of a market is based on the cross-price elasticity of demand among products to determine a certain group of products. For example, a measure of this is the small but significant and non-transitory increased in price test, namely the SSNIP test. It tests whether a hypothetical monopolist would shift demand to an alternative product if it increased its price by, say, 5–10%. However, whether these platform giants discussed in these cases can be seen as having market dominance requires further discussion, since the substantial reasonableness of the consideration in these transactions should be regulated as the subject of the transaction, for example, the provision of information or the possibility of purchase.

This is unlikely to be an issue that should be discussed when building a data distribution market. Businesses in the data market have so far varied from data originating from individuals to data from IoT devices, and monetization in the exchange function is still being explored (Hayashi and Ohsawa 2020). In addition, by discussing the competition issues of major IT companies, the business implication is that monetization from data distribution itself may not have been attempted. In other words, the difficulty in drawing market lines, which is a competition law enforcement issue, means that monetization from the transactions themselves is not direct, and is one of the possibilities for development from reality. On the other hand, the social implication is that it has become necessary to consider and make sense of the social and economic welfare of data distribution itself, the formation of market dominance in a non-monetized form, and the extent to which the maintenance and strengthening of market dominance should be subject to regulation.

4.2 Presumption of Monopoly Power

Second, it is necessary to consider whether the presumption of monopoly power holds. In both cases, it is clear that Google and Facebook would have dominant market shares if their respective markets were delineated. However, it is also clear that barriers to entry vary from service to service, that the cost of providing similar services on the Internet may not be significant, that the services offered on the Internet are changing significantly, and that (direct and indirect) network effects affect the inducement to trade. The following are some of the reasons why this is the case. It could be argued that market share does not directly imply monopoly power.

In recent years, there has been a proliferation of studies analyzing issues related to two-sided (multi-sided) markets from a competition policy perspective. For example, in the U.S. Supreme Court decision in the Amex case (Ohio v. American Express Co., 138 S. Ct. 2280 (2018)), the market definition approach of separating merchants versus market and cardholders versus market and demarcating them as one relevant market rather than as separate relevant markets was discussed. The decision was 5–4 in favor of this approach, but academic views were divided.

Thus, it may be necessary to explain and prove how Google and Facebook have monopoly power, not only in terms of market share, but especially from a dynamic perspective.

This has ambivalent implications from the perspective of data distribution market construction. On the one hand, it may ensure the possibility of occupying the benefits of data distribution, encourage innovation, promote new entrants, and invigorate the data distribution market. On the other hand, it could also lead to the emergence of operators with market-dominating power, which could impede market development and stall technological innovation. In order to be presumed to have market dominance, an entity must have the power to control prices freely to some extent in the market. However, it is not required to actually raise or lower prices. It is also required that the price increase or decrease be continuous for a certain period of time, rather than temporary. One characteristic of data distribution markets is the network effect: the more people trading, the more attractive the market becomes, and the more likely it is to lead to market dominance. On the other hand, the greater the volume of data, the more attractive the market becomes, which may promote a certain level of open data distribution rather than enclosure in a specific data format. Therefore, the practical implications of the presumption of market dominance as a matter of competition law are that major IT companies have overcome major market transitions and have secured a certain amount of profit sharing potential. As a social implication, it is necessary to consider adopting such a method in order to develop the data distribution market. In addition, it is necessary to prepare for flexible certification of market dominance and flexible law enforcement based on the size of demand and overall business capacity, not just current market share.

4.3 Actions to Form, Maintain, and Strengthen Market Dominance

Third, it is necessary to identify acts of forming, maintaining, and strengthening market dominance. Regarding unreasonable exclusion, for example, stating in a contractual provision that the company will not do business with business competitors, rather than explicitly excluding others, is not in itself an unreasonable exclusion. In a discussion of competition law, the mere existence of a monopoly is not in itself illegal. A monopoly based on market dominance violates the law only when it leads to acts of suppression of competition, such as exclusion of others or market closure. In this sense, it is difficult to distinguish how unreasonable exclusion is made from mere offensive competition measures. Aggressive promotions, defensive contracts, and various devices to increase the likelihood of monetization and occupancy are, in fact, paper-thinly different from exclusionary conduct.

The mutual perceptions of both parties should be the subject of evidence. Not only must it be shown that the conduct was artificial (intentional), but also how the potential parties to the transaction perceived it and how restrictive the provision was. The question is how behavior changed as a result of its inclusion as compared to its absence. Of course, several factors must be judged in totality, and careful discussion of the effects of the contractual provisions, the target of the acquisition, the use of consumer information, and other factors is desirable.

In exercising market dominance, several points need to be considered in establishing a data distribution market. In establishing a data distribution market, the difficulty of monetization and the need for possibilities of possession must be fully considered, and exclusionary acts by others and market closure must be prevented. There are two ways to deal with this. On the one hand, typical exclusionary acts by others include various types of restrictive agreements, coercive acts, and predatory acts. Market-closing acts include obstruction of new market entry, obstruction of the development of new business partners, and monitoring and intervention in the behavior of others. On the other hand, excluding others and ensuring the possibility of occupying the profits of the established market has a certain legitimacy in business. Excessive or artificial barriers will impede the development of data distribution markets. A balance must be struck between allowing monetization (to promote ingenuity) and prohibiting it (as a precautionary measure), taking both of these perspectives into account.

One key to striking this balance is whether the conduct contributes to the expansion of demand and expands the market as a whole. If it merely benefits only those who engage in the restrictive conduct, it would need to be more rigorously justified; if it expands the size of the market as a whole, it would not need to be justified. The criterion for judgment would be whether the act contributes to an increase in overall market demand beyond the company's own sales, or whether it merely takes sales from other companies.

The social implications of the issue of acts to form, maintain, and strengthen market dominance related to the establishment of a data market are difficult to determine because of the importance of encouraging the ingenuity of businesses for monetization and preventing highly malicious acts for the development of the market. In contrast, in practical terms, the primary implication is to consider and adopt strategies for the development of a certain data distribution market to increase the overall market demand. In addition, while some actions are prohibited, from a business perspective, it is important to first take a variety of proactive measures.

4.4 Harm to Consumers

Fourth, it is necessary to consider whether consumers have been substantially harmed. Of course, the stifling of innovation and the possibility of consumer choice must be taken into account in competition law enforcement. However, the principle of competition law is that if competition is restricted, the law has been violated. It does not matter whether the damage is caused or not. The destruction of the competitive mechanism of the market itself constitutes a violation of the law. However, this is a matter of legal dogma, and in the field of actual law enforcement, especially when discussing law enforcement against giant corporations, the important issue is how much damage was actually caused to consumers.

Also, factors such as increased efficiency, expanded functionality, and improved service quality would be factors to be considered. In addition to these factors, the increase in the number of consumers and the expansion of the market should also be evaluated. In other words, the expansion of search demand through the provision of appropriate search services, the development of the market through the provision of appropriate search advertising, and the extent to which social networking services for individuals, which were not previously widespread, have become a part of daily life. It is necessary to properly assess the loss of consumer surplus. Even when considering the loss of consumer surplus, it may be difficult to consider that surplus is decreasing when prices are decreasing (free) and demand is expanding.

In terms of the practical implications of this data distribution related to consumer damage, one of the most important aspects of the overall development of the monetized data market is how to realize consumer benefits beyond legal discussions and how to communicate those benefits to consumers. The ability to communicate the benefits to customers in a tangible way is an important factor for the development of the market, and is likely to have a significant impact on the legal debate and become more important in practice. In terms of social implications, this passing on and return of benefits to consumers may be cited as a performance indicator for measures that support the development of data markets. The fact that competition policy seeks to achieve this through competition also supports this implication, as it is ultimately in the interest of consumers.

4.5 Remedies

Fifth is a discussion of the need for antitrust action and measures to resolve the problem. Generally, a finding of illegality, an injunction against conduct, and future inaction are argued. To what extent are structural measures (e.g., so-called corporate divestitures) considered? For example, in the Microsoft litigation of the 2000s, Microsoft argued that the OS business (Windows) and the application business (Word and Excel) were complementary to each other, and after the monopoly was recognized, arguments for splitting these businesses emerged when considering the removal of monopoly power. Ultimately, however, this was not the case, and only behavioral measures were taken. In the future, structural measures may also be considered in this manner, depending on the arguments in the litigation.

A characteristic feature of competition law enforcement is that it is a problem-solving measure. Litigation often ends, in principle, with an injunction or an order for damages. However, in competition law litigation, if there is a violation of the law, not only is an injunction of certain conduct or an order for damages for the violation ordered, but also measures to restore the competitive status may be required. As the target of law enforcement is the market as a whole, necessary measures to ensure competition in the market will be required.

The practical implication of examining solutions to problems from the perspective of building a data distribution market is that it is necessary to be fully aware of the competitive situation in the market, and furthermore, when promoting monetization and market expansion in the data market, it is important to be aware of the existence of competitors and to consider the expansion of demand for oneself and the market as a whole. In terms of social implications, while it is important to crack down on individual anticompetitive means in order to build a data distribution market, it is also necessary to consider measures with an eye to the overall competitive order.

4.6 Communication Among Competitors

Other acts regulated as joint activities under the Antimonopoly Act are illegal if they restrict competition by, for example, raising prices through communication among competitors. In this case, if competition-related communication takes place between competitors and some agreement is reached, it is a violation of the Antimonopoly Act even if there is no price increase or other action taken. In the digital market, there are two issues. One is parallel price increases and the other is algorithmic cartels.

Parallel price increases mean that prices are raised in parallel without communication among competitors, which is not considered a problem under competition law. However, as prices become more transparent, especially in the digital market, it is possible that some action may be problematic in these situations.

As for algorithmic cartels and AI cartels/joint actions, although simulation studies have pointed out their potential, based on the suggestions from theoretical and experimental and empirical studies of actual pricing behavior, the time constraints, stability of the competitive environment, asymmetry of operators, and other simulation. Taking into account the limitations of the research and the meta-view from the results of other research methods that go beyond it, it may be difficult to immediately see how this could be a major problem for competition in certain trading areas. However, it is a new problem, with dangers being pointed out from various angles.

5 Conclusion

In this chapter, we have attempted to summarize the issues involved in facilitating the distribution of data, how large platform operators conduct their economic activities in the marketplace, and how they are actually regulated and dealt with. In particular, we briefly examined the actual antitrust litigation in the U.S. and summarized the issues. The U.S. DOJ's lawsuits against Google are, first, to prevent Google from monopolizing (intentionally creating and maintaining monopoly power) general search services, second, to prevent Google from monopolizing search advertising, and third, to prevent Google from monopolizing general search text advertising. The U.S. FTC's actions against Facebook are, first, to prevent Facebook from neutralizing an important independent competitor in personal social networking services through its acquisition and continued dominance of Instagram; second, to prevent Facebook from neutralizing a significant competitive threat to Facebook's monopoly in personal social networking through its acquisition and continued control of Whatsapp; third, to prevent Facebook from limiting the competitive threat to Facebook's monopoly in personal social networking by imposing anti-competitive conditions on access to the API platform available to Facebook app developers.

Against these we can argue from five perspectives. First, we emphasize the delineation of the relevant market, which is also the first entry point in the competition analysis. Second, the existence of monopoly power requires an analysis of barriers to entry and the transition of dominant firms. Third, the analysis of the act of forming, maintaining, or strengthening market dominance is at the core of the anti-competitive determination. The criterion for this determination is whether the conduct contributes to the expansion of demand in the market as a whole beyond the company's own sales, or whether it merely deprives other companies of sales. Fourth, it is necessary to consider whether the conduct has caused substantial harm to consumers. Fifth, it is necessary to consider the appropriateness of antitrust action, resolution of the problem, and remedy. Besides these points, it is necessary to consider communication between competitors for joint actions.

References

Hayashi, T, Ohsawa Y (2020) Data market business trends and the growth of data trading ecosystem. In: The 34th annual conference of the Japanese society for artificial intelligence, 1F5-OS-4-04

Matsushima N (2021) Factors harming competition in digital platform markets. Annu Jpn Assoc Econ Law 42:98–110

Shibata J (2021) The significance of regulation on abuse of superior bargaining position for digital platforms. Annu Jpn Assoc Econ Law 42:40–60

Takeda K (2021) Digital platforms and exclusionary conduct. Annu Jpn Assoc Econ Law 42:17–39

Vande Walle S (2021) Competition law and digital platforms: are remedies and commitments effective? Annu Jpn Assoc Econ Law 42:77–97

Wakui R (2021) Digital platforms and merger regulation. Annu Jpn Assoc Econ Law 42:61–76

Chapter 2
International Cooperation and Harmonization in Competition Law

1 Introduction

One of the pillars of competition law in the digital age is the big tech initiatives, which are undertaken primarily in developed countries such as the U.S., EU, and Japan. Another major goal is to facilitate the development of a digital economy and society through broad dissemination and awareness of competition law. From this perspective, this chapter could be viewed as an overview of the authors' efforts to promote competition law in emerging economies.

The main purpose of this chapter is to demonstrate the importance of legal assistance for developing countries in Asia, especially East and Southeast Asia. Section 2 describes the progress made in the countries including Central Asia (Uzbekistan), East Asia (Mongolia and China), and Southeast Asia (Vietnam and Cambodia) over the past decade. In these countries, the status of economic development and the development of economic and social capital are still different from those in developed countries. People's understanding of market competition is also more ambiguous than that in developed countries. At the same time, the extent and form of the introduction of competition law as well as its enforcement vary significantly.

Market competition is generally to be seen as a beneficial social mechanism for achieving efficiency in resource allocation in Asian developing countries. However, there have been periods in which competition was restricted by public policy measures on grounds of fairness of distribution in these countries. The trade-off between efficiency and fairness often brings about economic systems with policy management that emphasizes distributional fairness over market competition, as symbolized by various policy measures to promote specific industry sectors and to protect domestic industries.

The original version of this chapter was revised in the Reference section. A correction to the chapter can be found at
https://doi.org/10.1007/978-981-99-5310-3_12

S. Hayashi and K. Arai, *Digitalization and Competition Policy in Japan*,
https://doi.org/10.1007/978-981-99-5310-3_2

Moreover, such industrial policy measures often cause the existence of a collaborative network between interest groups and policy makers, involving tendencies toward favoritism and cronyism. In Japan, there are problems of bid rigging and collusive bidding at the initiative of government agencies. In developing countries, however, government corruption has caused serious social problems. Especially in Asia, where many countries started developing late and only at the initiative of the government, resistance to government market intervention is often weak, and the exclusive and discretionary nature of administrative powers persists.

In addition, social cushioning and control mechanism against the exploitation of consumers by domestic enterprises are still weak. In particular, the judiciary, which is supposed to protect the rights of citizens, is often powerless or involved in corruption. However, the main purpose of this chapter is not to discuss solutions for the problems of corruption and exploitation. Rather, these problems were mentioned because their existence is a fact that has to be taken into consideration when dealing with international cooperation and legal assistance in Asia, in particular in the field of competition law.

2 Current Situation and Need for Support of Competition Law Improvement in Asia

In the rapidly developing Asian market, the introduction and improvement of competition law and competition policy are increasing rapidly. A good example is the enactment of China's Anti-Monopoly Law in 2007. The development of competition law and policy in the East Asian region has been observed in the last two decades. In order to facilitate the development of the East Asian market and to enable competition law and policy to take its competitive environment into account, "legal assistance" from developed countries in Asia in the field of competition law is indispensable. In respect of this issue, Japan has the competition authority with the world's most experience in the administration of competition law, and is the top-ranked country in East Asia that provides technical support for developing countries. The problem lies in how to establish effective technical support systems based on the needs of the recipient country. Countries in the East Asian region are truly heterogeneous, with competition law structures that differ among countries and regions. Some countries and regions only have under-developed competition regulatory regimes, while others have sound competition laws and have accumulated much experience in competition law enforcement. The level of development and the need for legal assistance thus vary.

First, for example, South Korea (which codified its competition law in 1980 in the "Monopoly Regulation and Fair Trade Act") and Taiwan (which codified its competition law in 1992 in its "Fair Trade Act") have sufficient experience in the administration of competition law, whilst Japan is experienced in competition law administration and has already become a provider of knowledge and experience on competition law issues. Cooperation is thus necessary among providing countries ("donors") as well as between providing countries and receiving countries ("recipients"), so as to avoid "competition for legal assistance", which would result in contradicting each other's national interests.

Second, competition regulations and guidelines have been undergoing development for more than fifteen years since the codification of the competition laws in Thailand (in 1999) and Indonesia (in 2000). Despite the fact that the number of cases is rather small, positive achievements have been made in law enforcement, but these have been mainly limited to the area of unfair trade practices. For these countries, in order to improve competition law enforcement on other types of anticompetitive conduct, including cartels and abuse of a dominant position, practicable technical cooperation is required, such as a joint analysis of actual cases and of investigation methods.

Third, notable development of major regulations and guidelines has been observed in Vietnam (which codified its competition law in 2005), Mongolia (codified in 2005), and Laos (codified in 2004) since the introduction and initial enforcement of the competition acts. However, it is still insufficient.

The content of "legal assistance" could be quite different depending on the situation of the respective recipient country. According to Hiroshi Matsuo (H. MATSUO, Good Governance and the Rule of Law, in: Japan Reviewer 2009, 36), legal development support could be divided into three categories: (1) the enactment of adequate laws and regulations; (2) the establishment or improvement of governmental organs including legislative, administrative and judicial bodies; and (3) the training and education of lawyers and citizens. It includes a wide range of activities, ranging from general measures aiming at the development of society to the establishment and equipping of specific physical facilities to support the operation of the legal system and the conducting of surveys before and after the implementation of individual projects.

As a whole, these developing countries' progress in law enforcement is still poor when compared to Japan. Therefore, technical cooperation aiming for full-fledged implementation of competition law (such as support for the drafting of regulations and guidelines, for improving investigation methods, and for enforcing the law) is necessary, as is support for the build-up of an organizational framework that facilitates effective law enforcement.

Fourth, in countries with inadequate competition laws such as the Philippines (where competition law was codified only recently in 2016), Malaysia (codified in 2010), and Cambodia (comprehensive competition law is not yet developed), overall technical cooperation, such as teaching legal theory and assisting in building the capacity of law enforcement institutions, is needed in order to support the drafting of adequate legislation.

As mentioned below, the Japan Fair Trade Commission (JFTC) has been undertaking technical cooperation with overseas competition authorities based on the development assistance programs proposed by the Japan International Cooperation Agency (JICA). Such technical cooperation includes group training courses, counterpart training courses, long-term training, and country-/area-specific training courses.

However, the person in charge of the JFTC projects (the International Division of the Secretariat of the General Affairs Bureau in particular) maps out and implements the projects "ad hoc" for each separate training project, instead of implementing projects with a comprehensive perspective. The ad hoc approach, however, has its limits in implementing effective technical cooperation. In other words, for medium-to-long-term technical cooperation, it is time for the JFTC to start to develop "strategies" of legal assistance to determine recipients' demand and the forms of cooperation that should be carried out. Based on developed strategies, it is also necessary to consider the optimal project designs for the various recipient countries. Some countries in East and Southeast Asia, such as China and Indonesia, have already gone through the first stage of the development of competition law. The level of experience and competence of the competition authorities' officials who have participated in training programs offered by Japan is constantly improving. The technical cooperation programs have to be raised to a higher level in order to meet the needs of recipient countries.

In view of these issues in regard to the planning and design of overseas technical cooperation in the future, it is necessary to comprehensively analyze the needs of the recipient countries, the forms of feasible technical support Japan can provide, and the legal assistance provided by Western foreign countries.

For example, in the United States, the FTC and the DOJ have been making good use of the US Agency for International Development (USAID), and have provided programs that aim for a diversity of technical cooperation. In addition, it is urgent to shape the direction of medium- to-long-term legal assistance concerning Japan's competition policy.

3 "Fairness" in Asian Competition Laws

Based on the authors' experiences of being dispatched to numerous developing countries in Asia for legal assistance projects, it seems unpromising to introduce a US model of competition law and policy that mainly focuses on free competition. As Adam Smith said, efficiency could be achieved with individuals pursuing their own interests, as if led by the "invisible hand" of god. However, Smith was not particularly concerned with the question of how social justice could be attained through the market. His point was to emphasize that market competition would contribute to the achievement of economic efficiency. With respect to the legal assistance provided to more than 50 countries over the past fifteen years, assistance projects have been implemented in Central Europe, Eastern Europe, the former Soviet Union, Latin America, the Caribbean, and South Africa, and Asia has also been included as a target region in recent years. Four types of technical cooperation can be identified:

(1) dispatch of local experts (resident advisor), (2) short-term missions (one to two weeks), (3) organizing local conferences, (4) providing internships (see FTC, US Federal Trade Commission's and Department of Justice's Experience with Technical Assistance for the Effective Application of Competition Laws (6 February 2008), at http://www.ftc.gov/oia/wkshp/index.shtm). Among the mentioned types, the long-

term dispatch of experts usually draws the most attention, and is generally recognized as the most effective legal assistance. The FTC and DOJ sent experts to Eastern Europe from 1991 to 2001, to Argentina and South Africa in the late 1990s, and to Indonesia and the ASEAN Secretariat in 2001. The length of a local stay per expert is about half a year to one year. By dispatching multiple experts at different times, it seems possible for each authority to have experts stay for a total period of two years.

Regarding legal assistance of the United States, the acceptance of internships attracts attention as an approach that does not exist in Japan. In the past, regarding the acceptance of internships, the United States were inattentive due to confidentiality issues, but since the enactment of the US SAFE WEB Act in 2006, it seems that the FTC have been experimentally accepting trainees from the competition authorities of Brazil and Hungary, as well as from the consumer protection authorities of Canada. However, there is a problem that internships have to be limited to a small number of people due to the costs involved, the English proficiency of the trainees and other reasons. Japan has also accepted personnel from foreign competition authorities as trainees, but only exceptionally. Although there are many challenges to overcome due to the problems of confidentiality, training costs, Japanese language proficiency of trainees, etc., it is worth considering accepting more interns at the JFTC.

In Asia, however, the legal assistance in the context of competition law cannot be done without considering "the fairness of competition." After all, it took more than thirty years for the Antimonopoly Act to become rooted in Japan. To transplant a legal system only because it is from a developed country usually does not have support from the citizens in the recipient country, and, as a natural result, it does not root itself in the country.

The authors also believe that traditional competition law and policy can solve problems only in a very limited manner. As a matter of fact, severe social problems such as environmental pollution and labor exploitation lie ahead. The current challenging issue is how to respond to corporate social responsibility and establish connections with other laws, such as labor law, in the context of economic law theory.

One of the features of competition law in Asia is the emphasis on regulating unfair trade practices. Likewise, regulations regarding the abuse of a superior bargaining position are another distinctive feature. In Asia, there is a general tendency to consider that ensuring fair trade (protection of competitors) is more important than ensuring free competition (protection of competition).

In East Asia, laws regulating only unfair trade practice were generally enacted prior to the enactment of more comprehensive competition laws. In South Korea, for example, the Unfair Competition (unfair trade practice) Prevention and Trade Secret Protection Act was enacted in 1961, and the Monopoly Regulation and Fair Trade Act was enacted later in 1980. In China, the (first) Law against Unfair Competition, which regulated only unfair trade practices, was enacted in 1993, and the Anti-Monopoly Law followed in 2008.

Further, in Taiwan, the prohibitively high license fee demanded by the patent pool for CD-R technology, which was actually set by Sony and Philips, was ruled abusive and declared illegal by the Taiwan Fair Trade Commission (TFTC). As another example, the TFTC also found the high price for Microsoft's software to be abusive and ordered remedies based on reconciliation proceedings.

Professor Ohseung Kwon (Seoul National University, Korea) has pointed out that it is easier to understand the meaning of fair trade than that of free competition (efficiency) in Eastern Asia, and there is a tension between the two (see O. KWON, Factors obstructing the Establishment of a Competitive Order, in: Kobe Law Journal 55(1) (June 2005) 9–12). Regarding the tension between free and fair competition, the example of tie-in sales as an unfair trade practice is easy to understand. Tie-in sales, from the perspective of competitors of secondary products, take away opportunities to compete, and harms competition that focuses on the low price and high quality of products. In contrast, from the viewpoint of free competition, the issue is whether the competitive process of the market for secondary products, which is outside the relationship of individual, is distorted or not.

There also should not be such a dichotomy between the "nation" and the "market". As was visible during the Asian currency crisis, the question lies in whether market mechanisms could protect the Asian regional "community" from the uncontrollable rampant effects of worldwide excessive capital liquidity. In this regard, maintaining free competition as a goal in East and Southeast Asia has to be seen in connection with the goal of maintaining fair trade.

4 Conclusion: Universalism and Particularism in Asian Competition Laws

Basically, competition law and social institutions originate from Europe and the United States. Competition laws in these countries should be evaluated with consideration of the whole social and political system, instead of simply separately. Although Asian legal systems are mostly inherited from Western laws, much of the "living law" has its origins in (the traditional culture of) pre-modern times. After all, there are differences between Asian countries and Western countries. With that being said, how should we weave these differences into the theory of competition law?

The authors would like to adopt a compromise approach to explain this matter. Given the differences in trade practices among countries, when applying the law, we must wisely take into account the importance of the principal values of Asian competition laws, which emphasize the protection of fair trade. Meanwhile, the overall frameworks of the competition laws in the United State and in Europe, where a US-style competition law had been originally adopted, have developed independently and differently. Thus, they cannot be simply seen as one model. Furthermore, another significant point is to distinguish between how the legal principle of competition law has developed and how individual competitors are affected. Taking away the individual competitor's opportunity to compete with low-priced products of high quality is not so much the issue here. Even if some competitors lose their trade opportunities, as long as the competition in the secondary product market is active, there would be no problem. Although free and fair competition are two sides of the same coin, their relationship is tense at the same time.

At this point, the authors appreciate some of the trends set out by law and economics theories in current American antitrust law. However, this does not contradict the fact that the tools of analysis (theory and demonstration) developed by law and economics theories are extremely fascinating. For reference, L. KAPLOW / S. SHAVELL, Fairness versus Welfare (Harvard 2002); L. KAPLOW / C. SHAPIRO, Antitrust, in: Polinsky / Shavell (eds.), Handbook of Law and Economics, vol. 2 (Amsterdam 2007) 1073.

With respect to cross-border competition law cases, a conflict is likely to occur when a competition authority adopts a universal point of view and another looks at the case from a particularistic point of view. Then global harmonization might be the only means to integrate the two views into a general framework of a legal system. However, the authors' concern is whether or not global harmonization alone would suffice. After all, the current antitrust theory in the United States, which seems to neglect fair trade, is particular to the United States and should not be seen as universal. Even in the United States, there has even been a period in which the survival of farmers and small and medium-sized producers was considered important (i.e. the atomistic market structure was considered important) to protect social health (the so-called "Jeffersonian democracy"). From a historical point of view, thus, we can never say that the emphasis on fair competition in Asia is exceptional and should be interpreted and applied with restraint.

In conclusion, the general supremacy of efficiency over social welfare in competition law today should be made less absolute based on the findings of regional studies of competition laws in Asia. Fair competition and fair trade should be given more emphasis, instead of being excluded as indicative of the backwardness of Asian competition laws. Legal assistance in the area of competition law in Asia also has to take this into account. In this regard, Japan's experience of regulating "unfair trade practices" can be a good example for other Asian countries. Such aspects are essential to establishing a common culture of competition in Asia.

5 Summary

Experience with various legal assistance projects for developing countries in Asia shows that the situation and level of development of competition law regimes differ greatly among these Asian countries. What kind of legal assistance in the field of competition law each such country needs therefore depends on the specific local situation. To improve legal assistance in Asia, the JFTC should develop a more sophisticated strategy of legal assistance for future medium-and-long-term assistance projects. It should also coordinate such projects better with other partners in Japan and with potential co-operation partners in other developed countries that also provide legal assistance to countries in Asia. Moreover, the specific needs, perceptions, and principal legal values of the recepient countries should to be taken into account more. In particular, legal assistance in Asia has to consider that there is a general tendency in many Asian countries to put more emphasis on fair competition than on free competition. It is therefore not promising to only implement Western models of competition law frameworks, which at present often prioritize ensuring free competition and efficient markets. In this regard, Japan can be a good example for many Asian countries, because the regulation of unfair trade practices is a very important part of Japanese competition law.

References

Aikyo M (2008) Nagoya University and Legal Assistance Project Study. Jurist 1358:17–25

Aikyo M (2011) What is legal assistance project? Nagoya University Press

Hayashi S (2010) Legal assistance concerning competition law in Asia. Fair Trade 715:23–28

Kaplow L, Shavell S (2002) Fairness versus welfare. Harvard University Press

Kaplow L, Shapiro C (2007) Chapter 15: Antitrust. In: Polinsky A M, Shavell S (eds) Handbook of law and economics, vol 2. North Holland, pp 1073–1225

Matsuo H (2009) Good governance and the rule of law: a challenge of law and development. Nippon Hyoron Sha

Obata T (2004) Development of competition laws in East Asian countries and technical assistance of the fair trade commission. International Economic Law (Annual Report of the Japan Association of International Economic Law) 13:37–54

Part II
Digital Initiatives in Japanese Competition Law

Part II of the book outlines discussions with respect to promoting competition in the digital sector, including approaches, methods, and evaluations. Along with this, it is observed that there has been an incremental but steady progress in enforcing competition law in the high-tech area.

Chapter 3
Big Data and AI

1 Introduction

Information distributed and processed on the ICT network continues expanding and diversifying as a result of the evolution and widespread of mobile devices and the progress of Internet of Things (IoT) technologies. Concerning the quantitative and qualitative expansion of information use, many advanced research projects have been undertaken for the purpose of understanding how to extract the value of data with big data analytics and AI-based technologies. The future vision of big data and AI is however not yet clearly defined. For example, how to connect big data and artificial intelligence (AI) with the ICT network and create new services, and how to enhance convenience for public with big data and AI through having machines working alongside people so that they could concentrate on creative works, are part of the coming issues associated with big data and AI. At the same time, security and privacy issues are becoming more of a concern to consumers.

In the ICT sector, mechanisms are under development to efficiently transmit small but various amounts of data, and to aggregate networks or apply distributed processing according to the load of Software Defined Network. In the fields of data processing and utilisation, AI developments have dramatically streamlined the data processing system, and new methods centered on cognitive process have become reality. However, there is a need for closer cooperation among the following ongoing developments: (1) accelerated improvement of the capacity of CPU, storage, and communication network, (2) advancement of AI, (3) conversion of everything into data, and (4) distributed data processing. Despite the scale of these developments, relatively limited research has been conducted from a social science viewpoint. In view of this, this chapter provides a preliminary analysis of an incoming ICT-based society from the perspective of competition law.

This chapter thus puts emphasis on how data and the Internet are connected, and aims to establish a basic analytical framework of the ICT-based technical coordination with particular focus on the competition stimulated by the prospect of 'AI networking'. This chapter looks at in what manner the AI network and competition

S. Hayashi and K. Arai, *Digitalization and Competition Policy in Japan*,
https://doi.org/10.1007/978-981-99-5310-3_3

ecosystem interact with each other in their development process. The authors also consider how to strengthen Japan's international competitiveness in this field, and propose some recommendations on future strategies.

2 Competition Stimulated by the Prospect of AI Network

2.1 Coordination and Competition in AI Network

How to facilitate coordination for the development of AI network while securing a competitive ecosystem is the main focus of this chapter. In this regard, traditional competition theories, e.g. platform competition, might have difficulties in properly explaining the arising competition across different layers of ICT network, and accordingly have an adverse effect on disruptive innovation and new value creation. This chapter thus is not intended to focus only on the application of competition regulations on AI or big data, but on a broader competitive scope, which may include innovative competition among AI-related industries.

Coordination is indispensable for the progress of AI network. Since the late twentieth century, the progress of AI network has been made thanks to the developments of information and communication technologies. These developments include: (1) advancement of sensor technology and audio/video recognition technology (perception device), (2) expansion of big data on the Internet, (3) development of advanced information processing technologies including machine learning techniques (deep learning), and (4) progress of artificial sound/image creation technology, robot technology, and realisation of AI-networked society. On the other hand, approaches adopted to secure a competitive ecosystem in all big data or AI-related markets are no less important but less discussed. To illustrate, a competitive ecosystem is a complex system composed of various players, including platform operators, engaging in R&D and investment in various big data or AI-related businesses. Such ecosystem requires strategic approaches to achieve coordination and competition inside the system. The purpose of this chapter is thus to figure out how to strike a balance between coordination and competition, two bipolar concepts in the context of competition law.

2.2 AI Platform

Before going through AI platform, this section will address the definition of AI networking and AI network. First, AI networking refers to the development of the AI network system, such as the construction of AI network system and cooperation between AIs. To simplify, AI networking means a phenomenon where AI systems connect to an information communication network (e.g. the Internet), and are utilised in conjunction with other AI and non-AI systems. Second, AI network refers to an information communication network system that includes an AI system connected to an information communication network, the information communication network itself, and other systems connected to the information communication network. Lastly, 'AI platform' is however the basis for mediating the functions of an AI network for other people through the ICT network. The concept of platform has not been defined in legal terms. However, the term 'platform' itself is widely used in various ways and scenarios without the concrete definitions. According to their installation patterns, platforms could be categorized into various types including a form to be implemented in the network, a form to be installed in devices, and a form in which connects devices and servers. These forms of implementation evolve rapidly, leading to a difficulty in defining the concept of platform. Even if the term was clearly defined, the actual concept of platform might be changed quickly over the time due to complex relationships with other markets and technological innovation.[1]

Irrespective of the concrete forms of implementation, this chapter deliberately avoid strictly defining the concept of AI platform. Many Cyber-Physical Systems (CPS),[2] based on IoT/Big Data/AI technologies, are established far and wide to analyze results of data collected from real space and then immediately give feedbacks to the real space automatically. For instance, by connecting AI systems with other systems, a collaborative infrastructure may possibly be applicable in the AI platform and enable the following benefits, including (1) utilisation of the AI system using the data output by the other systems, (2) usage of the data output by the AI system to operate the other systems, (3) usage of the AI system, (4) utilisation of the AI system operation from the other systems, (5) creating an advance functions by combining individual AI systems, and (6) data network effects—AI service becomes more highly intelligent by acquiring more data from the users via machine learning.

According to the Sect. 2.1, there are several stages in the development of AI. In the first stage, AI is commonly introduced into OTT platforms.[3] Nevertheless, the problem of data concentration may arise and lead to anti-competitive practices. In the second stage, other anti-competitive problems may subsequently occur including restriction of AI networking among AIs (refusal to cooperate, peer, etc.), discriminatory treatment in networking, anticompetitive merger or acquisition. In this chapter, all connected networks existing in the first and second stage are temporarily defined as platforms, and their core functions as AI platforms.

[1] With the convergence of telecommunications and broadcasting and the development of IoT, it is necessary to analyze whether the object functioning as a platform affects competition, and, if this is the case, such platform should be subjected to competition regulations.

[2] A cyber-physical system (CPS) is a mechanism that is controlled or monitored by computer-based algorithms, tightly integrated with the Internet and its users. In cyber-physical systems, physical and software components are deeply intertwined, each operating on different spatial and temporal scales, exhibiting multiple and distinct behavioural modalities, and interacting with each other in a myriad of ways that change with context. See, US National Science Foundation, 'Cyber-Physical Systems (CPS)'. https://www.nsf.gov/pubs/2010/nsf10515/nsf10515.htm. Accessed 6 January 2018.

[3] OTT (Over The Top) refers to businesses that provide contents or services, such as movies and music streaming services, via the Internet.

Big data will essentially be the key to competition. During our everyday life, we unexpectedly provide personal data through the usage of the Internet or even though search engines. This problem is however linked to many aspects including personal data protection, privacy law, unfair competition law and competition law. One of the potential problems is concentration of data on a specific AI platform, which could cause anti-competitive issues. Furthermore, problems may occur when most of the AI platforms are interconnected but an outsider company cannot connect to this huge network. Thus, this may lead to discrimination or deceit problems. In addition, if a market participant is not coordinating on AI networking matters, social welfare might be eventually affected and thus we need to pay particular attention upon this.

3 AI and Data Concentration

3.1 Anticompetitive Effects Resulting from Network Effects

Currently, there are numerous audio or video streaming websites (e.g. YouTube, Netflix, Spotify) which provide unlimited music and video streaming in exchange for collecting personal data unconsciously in various forms. A fierce competition of acquiring and collecting personal data is unfolded among major platform companies such as Google, Amazon, Facebook and Apple with a business model based on a multidirectional market that enables free market in exchange with acquiring data and make use of the big data they acquired (e.g. total quantity of data, ease of acquisition of real time data). Considering the competitive aspect, the network effect is firstly needed to be determined as there are many users engaging in the same common place—so called 'platform'.

Platform enhanced by network effect shall increase more value to both business industries and AI platform. Nevertheless, some concerns arise whether platforms with market dominance may have a competition-restrictive effect. The existence of the network effect is not harmful; however, the close attention may be needed, especially the entry barrier effect.

The data network effect is very essential to AI as the more users use AI services, the more data will be provided. As a result, the overall service will be enhanced. However, oligopolistic or monopolistic behaviours in AI platform may occur when the service providers acquire huge amount of data. In addition, AI system output or program may be changed by learning from the data acquired and this may lead to some difficulties, e.g. understanding, verification, and control.

3.2 Competition Issues in the Data-Driven Society

With the dissemination of AI technology, the fourth industrial revolution characterized by a fusion of advance technologies[4] is expected to create a data-driven society[5] in which data is the key to success in competition. However, it is yet unclear how to accurately evaluate the importance of data from a competition law perspective. Generally, the first step in a competition analysis is to delineate a relevant market where the anticompetitive effects occur. It is possible, for example, to imagine a scenario in which data (e.g. customer data collected by home appliance manufacturers) is the main target of a proposed merger, but the question that should be firstly asked and answered is whether data could be deemed to be the subject of a proposed transaction. Other possible scenarios include defining the relevant market as the market for data accumulation or storage and then determining whether a company's behaviour constitutes an abuse of its market power.

On the other hand, the question arises whether data could constitute to an 'essential facility' in the competition law context? Theoretically, it is possible, though not likely in practice, to consider data to be an 'essential facility' in specific circumstances.[6] For example, real-time data about the access to base stations, which could be collected only by wireless carriers, might be required for machine learning (e.g. to develop a sophisticated system capable of fully autonomous driving) and thus deemed to be an essential facility for competitors conducting R&D on AI algorithms. However, some concerns have been raised about the application of the essential facilities doctrine to data. For those dominant companies whose dominance is the result of efficient use of their accumulated data, their investment and R&D incentives would be reduced, or even eliminated, if their data or analytical tools are deemed to be essential facilities and made available to their competitors notwithstanding the fact that they collected the data or developed the analytics tools all by themselves. In view of such risk, prudence is thus necessary when a competition agency evaluates competition and market power regarding data-related competition concerns, and companies are recommended to analyse the value of data collected and owned by themselves from an integrated perspective of business strategy and competition law compliance.

---

[4] These technologies include IoT, cloud computing, machine-to-machine (M2M) communications, 3D printing, and big data.

[5] A data-driven society refers to a society in which data creates new value through cyber-physical systems, which are made possible by the development of communications technologies including M2M and IoT.

[6] For a detailed discussion on the possibility of applying the essential facilities doctrine to data, see Graef (2016).

4 Big Data, AI and Competition Law

The data-related competition issues create challenge to competition regulators in the digital economy. With the coming of the fourth industrial revolution, the issue of data and competition policy has become one of the most pressing competition concerns in a global context. Japanese government has begun to discuss data-related competition issues.[7] The Ministry of Economy, Trade and Industry (METI), having jurisdiction over Japan's industrial policies, established 'Study Group for Ideal Approaches to Competition Policies for the Fourth Industrial Revolution' and published a study report in 2017.[8] Meantime, the Japan Fair Trade Commission (JFTC) established 'Study Group on Data and Competition Policy' to clarify the competition issues relating to accumulation and use of data, and also published a study report.[9] The similar trend is observed in academic discussions. *Big data and Competition Policy*,[10] a first-of-its-kind book discussing the issues of data monopolies, attracted much attention on its publication in 2016 and has been frequently referred to by competition law scholars all over the world, including Japan. This section will then focus on the following six topics in the context of data accumulation and use, trying to depict a whole picture of the issues: market power, market definition, abuse of dominance, merger review, protection of personal data and competition policy, and data ownership and data portability.

4.1 *Market Power in Data-Related Markets: How to Measure It?*

The most relevant determinant of a company's market power in a data-related market is the volume of data it possesses. The possession of big data might strengthen market power for it ensures a company's competitiveness on the market, irrespective of whether the product or service provided to customers is free or not. Yet so far there is no consensus about how to define a relevant market and qualitatively or quantitatively measure market power in a data-related competition analysis. Apart from the difficulties arising directly from the intangible nature of data, another concern is that there are various types of data, such as online transaction data, which can be used

[7] For a discussion on big data and related competition issues raised by French and German competition agencies, see Autorité de la concurrence German and Bundeskartellamt, *Competition Law and Data* (2016). www.autoritedelaconcurrence.fr/doc/reportcompetitionlawanddatafinal.pdf. Accessed 19 December 2017.

[8] Ministry of Economy, Trade and Industry, *Report of the Study Group for Ideal Approaches to Competition Policies for the Fourth Industrial Revolution—Towards the realization of Connected Industries* (Provisional translation, 2017). www.meti.go.jp/english/press/2017/pdf/0628_001b.pdf. Accessed 19 December 2017.

[9] Japan Fair Trade Commission, *Report of Study Group on Data and Competition Policy* (Tentative translation, 2017). www.jftc.go.jp/en/pressreleases/yearly-2017/June/170606.files/170606-4.pdf. Accessed 19 December 2017.

[10] Stucke and Grunes (2016).

to identify customers, and real-time spatial data indispensable for the IoT. Different types of data have different uses and values, which may also vary depending on the sector where the data owner operates. All these things make the market power issue more complex.

Many data-related markets involve zero-price products or services. Companies generally provide zero-price products or services in exchange for data. However, traditional methods of market definition (such as hypothetical monopolist test) often reveal themselves as inoperative in assessing market power in these markets. Even if modified traditional methods might be found operable in some cases, such methods are likely to lead to an underestimate of market power in specific circumstances.[11] It is important to note that the offer of zero-price products or services may be part of a profit-maximising business strategy to attract price-sensitive consumers.[12] Companies may employ such strategy to accrue market power, and then exercise the power over other customers (e.g. consumers paying for the products or services) or even leverage the market power into another market.[13]

On the other hand, 'data is new currency.' To illustrate, personal data has become the most valuable currency in today's information economy. It thus stands to reason, to some extent, to compare the expanding collection of personal data to the increasing price of personal data.[14] Another related point of view is that consumers substantially pay for the zero-price products or services (e.g. internet search services with information created or inputted by themselves such as search keywords). The collection and use of data may in principle promote consumer welfare by providing better customized services to consumers; however, due to data network effects it might form a feedback loop of data and profit. Such feedback loop raises competition concerns where it could make big companies bigger and thus create barriers to market entry.

The possession of data does not necessarily endow a company with market power. In some circumstances, data possession is a prerequisite to provide innovative services, which might encourage and stimulate market competition. It is imaginable however that the possession of data might lead to the forming, maintaining or strengthening of market power under the following circumstances[15]: (1) A company

[11] Collyer et al. (2017).

[12] Organisation for Economic Co-operation and Development (OECD), *Big data: Bringing competition policy to the digital era* (DAF/COMP(2016)14) para 48. https://one.oecd.org/document/DAF/COMP(2016)14/en/pdf. Accessed 19 December 2017.

[13] For example, a nightclub might throw a ladies night where women can get in free and enjoy free drinks but men need to pay the full cover charge. In this case, the nightclub is a two-sided market, the mechanism of which attracts and links different groups of customers (male and female customers). The nightclub owner would build its market power with this mechanism and then exert the power over the group of male customers.

[14] Organisation for Economic Co-operation and Development (OECD), *Big data: Bringing competition policy to the digital era* (DAF/COMP(2016)14) para 56. https://one.oecd.org/document/DAF/COMP(2016)14/en/pdf. Accessed 19 December 2017.

[15] Competition and Markets Authority, *The Commercial Use of Consumer Data—Report on the CMA's Call for Information* (CMA38, 2015) para 3.73. www.gov.uk/government/uploads/system/uploads/attachment_data/file/435817/The_commercial_use_of_consumer_data.pdf. Accessed 19 December 2017.

engages in exclusionary conduct as a way of preventing competitors from accessing and using data, e.g. by means of exclusive licences, exclusive dealing arrangements and/or other controlling methods. (2) Dominant companies exist in a data-related market and new entrants have difficulties in accessing or collecting data due to the cost structure. (3) The mechanism of two-sided market works in the relevant market, and links between the two or multi sides of the market are strong, particularly in cases where consumers are single homing. These circumstances involve a risk of generating barriers to market entry and thus raise competition concerns.

4.2 Market Definition

Digital platforms, represented by Google, Amazon, Facebook, Apple (GAFA), are blooming and have become dominant in one or more market industries. These successful platform-based high-tech companies have demonstrated that key factors determining a company's market position in the digital economy are no longer natural resources or other traditional production factors, but data and innovation. The massive collection of data, as input goods for digital platforms, contributed to the strengthening of a company's market position in many service markets. In light of the value of data, scholars and practitioners have proposed to delineate a relevant data market so as to adequately measure ongoing competition among digital platforms.[16] However, competition agencies would face difficulties in defining such relevant market due to the lack of enforcement experience in the field associated with data or AI.

Concerning the available quantitative tools for delineating data or AI-related markets, the first step is to figure out what product or service is offered, who demands and who supplies the product or service. It is nevertheless difficult because, unlike typical situations, traditional market definition tools, such as a small but significant and non-transitory increase in price (SSNIP) test, are not applicable and need to be modified to fit the particular conditions of a data or AI-related market. Many data or AI-related markets are two or multi-sided markets, and contain at least one side that involves zero-price offers. Traditional market definition tools are thus not useful due to their dependence on the price of a product or service. A small but significant non-transitory decrease in quality (SSNDQ) test might be a potential solution, but is so far considered inoperable in practice.[17] In view of the fact that data or AI-related markets

[16] For example, former FTC Commissioner Pamela Jones Harbour noted in her dissenting opinion in the matter of Google/Doubleclick that, "The Commission is uniquely situated to evaluate the implications of this kind of data merger, from a competition as well as a consumer protection perspective. The Commission should maximize its opportunity to do so, especially where the merged firm will be capable of dominating the 'Database of Intentions.'" See, Harbour (2007, p. 4).

[17] 'The SSNDQ test faces criticism that in practice it is unworkable, however, given the inherent difficulties of measuring quality alongside the existing complications of the applying the SSNIP test itself within real market situations. See, Organisation for Economic Co-operation and Development (OECD), *The Role and Measurement of Quality in Competition Analysis* (DAF/COMP(2013)17) 9. www.oecd.org/competition/Quality-in-competition-analysis-2013.pdf. Accessed 10 January 2018.

are complicated ecosystems involving a collection of various data sets derived from multiple products and services, competition agencies would find it difficult, if not impossible, to objectively identify and measure the correlation between data quality and competition.[18] Moreover, the quality of a product or service is a subjective factor and has different dimensions depending on the purposes of use. Competition agencies would face the challenge of deciding which parameters should be taken into account when delineating a data-related relevant market. A similar dilemma emerges in the case of a small but significant and non-transitory increase in costs (SSNIC) test.[19]

4.3 *Abuse of Dominance: Could Data Constitute an 'Essential Facility'?*

Examples of abuse of market power in a data-related market include: (1) obstructing or denying the rival's access to essential data sets; (2) preventing rivals from accessing data through exclusive agreements with data providers so that the data cannot be shared or transferred; (3) leveraging its dominant market power, which results from the possession of data, into another market so as to exclude rivals. Regarding abuse of market power, German and French competition agencies suggested in a joint report that the essential facilities doctrine is in principle applicable to data. Refusal to access to data can be anticompetitive if the data are an "essential facility" to the activity of the undertaking asking for access.[20] According to ECJ precedents,[21] the essential facilities doctrine would be theoretically applicable if the data possessed by a firm is unique, indispensable for carrying on the business in question, and if there are no alternative data and there are technical, legal or economic obstacles which make it impossible or unreasonably difficult for a competitor to obtain the data by itself. These requirements are however difficult to meet in practice, and no related decisions have been made so far. Yet with the rapid development of AI, it is possible, if not probable, that soon certain data sets would be indispensable for developing certain AI applications, e.g. connected devices equipped with AI.

[18] In addition, scholars have described some scenarios where competition and quality are not necessarily positively correlated. See, Ezrachi and Stucke (2015).

[19] The SSNIC test is developed based on the hypothetical monopolist test but replaces the price variable with the relevant information (which may include privacy) and/or attention costs of customers. That is, competition agencies apply the SSNIC test to see whether a hypothetical monopolistic firm would likely be able to profitably impose a small but significant and non-transitory increase in costs on customers. However there are many potential issues that can arise in practice. See, Newman (2016).

[20] Autorité de la concurrence German and Bundeskartellamt, *Competition Law and Data* (2016) 17. www.autoritedelaconcurrence.fr/doc/reportcompetitionlawanddatafinal.pdf. Accessed 19 December 2017.

[21] Case C-7/97, *Bronner v Mediaprint* [1998] ECR I-7791, paras 44–45; Case C-418/01, *IMS Health GmbH & Co. OHG v NDC Health GmbH & Co. KG* [2004] ECR I-5039, paras 34-52; Case T-201/04 *Microsoft v Commission* [2007] ECR II-3601, paras 320–336.

As described in 3.1, data network effects occur in AI businesses, where a vast amount of data is indispensable for performing machine learning (deep learning). It thus could be problematic if the data collected and possessed by a monopolistic incumbent is exclusively used, or if rival's access to such data is substantially restricted. In these exceptional circumstances, the monopolist's conduct might constitute a form of foreclosure of an essential input (data) and have anti-competitive effects. On the other hands, competition agencies need pay attention to concerns about competitor's free riding, and avoid impeding incentives to collect and use data. Especially, with respect to data that would not be under legal protection once it becomes open and accessible to competitors, competition agencies should be mindful of the free-riding concerns when imposing an obligation on a company to provide its competitors with access to the data it possesses, or when ordering a company to licence its data sets on fair, reasonable and non-discriminatory (FRAND) terms. Moreover, if a data set is protected by a company as its trade secret,[22] competition agencies need to take into account the potential conflict between competition and unfair competition law from an enforcement perspective.[23]

4.4 Standard for Merger Review: Does Privacy Constitute a Competition Concern?

The number of merger and acquisition cases, in which debates have occurred with respect to consumer privacy protection, is on the rise. Although there is no consensus on the introduction of a privacy dimension into competition policy, competition agencies may have a justification to address privacy as a competition concern.[24] There thus exists an urgent need for competition agencies to study and clarify whether there is any anti-competitive privacy-related practices existing in the data-oriented industry.

The collection and possession of consumer data may impose costs in form of the loss of privacy on consumers. Here is an imaginary scenario that illustrates the potential concerns inherent in data-related merger cases. A Japanese electronic appliance manufacturing company wants to sell its healthcare/medical device division to a foreign company. The division developed an electronic medical record system, which has been introduced into many hospitals in Japan, and keeps a backup of

[22] Agreement on Trade-Related Aspects of Intellectual Property Rights (TRIPs), art 39.

[23] Another related issue here is the possibility of market entry of new competitors. In the data-driven society, data network effects may lead to winner-takes-all outcomes, which makes it extremely difficult for any potential market participant to enter a data or AI-related market where dominant incumbents exist. It is however unclear how to quantitatively assess the possibility of market entry in a data or AI-related market, for the concept of competition in a data or AI-related market remains partly ambiguous as stated above.

[24] Organisation for Economic Co-operation and Development (OECD), *Big data: Bringing competition policy to the digital era* (DAF/COMP(2016)14) paras 55–56. https://one.oecd.org/document/DAF/COMP(2016)14/en/pdf. Accessed 19 December 2017.

all medical data. Briefly speaking, a data set containing Japanese patients' medical record would be put under the control of a foreign company if the acquisition is clear by competition authorities. Such scenario is usually associated with data protection concerns, but some competition agencies have begun to look at possible competition issues in similar scenarios.[25] A well-known case is the *Google/DoubleClick* merger. Pamela Jones Harbour, a former FTC Commissioner, has expressed her concerns in the dissenting statement of *Google/DoubleClick*,[26] enlightening the public from a privacy perspective in the context of competition policy.

"The parties claim to place a high value on protecting consumer privacy....I am uncomfortable accepting the merging parties' nonbinding representations at face value. The truth is, we really do not know what Google/DoubleClick can or will do with its trove of information about consumers' Internet habits....Traditional competition analysis of Google's acquisition of DoubleClick fails to capture the interests of all the relevant parties....this analysis does not reflect the values of the consumers whose data will be gathered and analyzed....there is no adequate proxy for the consumers whose privacy is at stake, because consumers have no business relationship with Google or DoubleClick."

4.5 Protection of Personal Data and Competition Policy

The utilisation of big data has raised grave concerns about consumer data privacy. There are however different views among countries on what approach—competition law or consumer(privacy) law—should be adopted to address these concerns. Competition Agencies, which are originally supposed to protect consumers, are facing challenges to enforce competition laws in the zero-price data market. The reason lies in the difficulty of measuring the direct economic damage by figures in the competition analysis. Also, as the premise of privacy protection, the definition of privacy is not definite in the first place. This is because privacy has multiple dimensions. Moreover, it is possible that the competition agency considers the issues of personal data not to fall under its jurisdiction, and leave them to the judgment of other agencies.

Assume that privacy protection is related to the competition law, to the authority, how to keep a balance between ensuring appropriate competition and protecting privacy is not clear. On one hand, when ensuring competition is given priority, protecting privacy is likely to become a matter that is not absolutely important anymore. On the other hand, do consumers have strong concern over the protection of their own privacy, or do they not care so much about privacy protection in the case of zero-price?

---

[25] There are however criticisms against introducing privacy into the merger review process as a relevant parameter of non-price competition, e.g., Ben Holles de Peyer 'EU MERGER CONTROL AND BIG DATA' Journal of Competition Law & Economics. https://doi.org/10.1093/joclec/nhx026. Accessed 20 January 2018.

[26] Harbour (2007, pp. 9–12).

Why has the agency not given enough consideration to the influence of big data? Because it is very difficult to add to the competition analysis the noneconomic damage caused by invasion of privacy, which is not connected to direct economic damage. Even if the authority gives clear consideration to the damage on privacy, the problem of how the authority or the court will keep a balance between the consideration of privacy and other interests specifically still remains.

The acquisition of *Facebook/Whatsapp*[27] will bring massive and a variety of data to the conglomerate in the future. Enterprises might make the data open to the public, or promise not to use it in behaviour targeting advertisements. However, if a merger increases market dominance, the enterprise might go back on its promises about privacy, and the level of privacy protection might go down. Assume that Whatsapp collects user data and only uses it within the company for the purpose of improving technical performances. Whatsapp users, after Facebook's acquisition, might be worried because Facebook can get access to their data at any time. It is possible that Facebook's acquisition of Whatsapp will impair people's sense of security with regards to personal data; however, such anxiety, or sense of insecurity, might not fall under the category of the privacy law. When personal data is used by the enterprise against that person's own will, the issue arises as to whether the authority should establish a complex economic analysis regarding the harm associated with privacy invasion. It might be difficult for the authority to substantiate issues of the insubstantial noneconomic damage caused by privacy invasion.

4.6 Data Ownership and Data Portability

Data ownership and data portability play an important role in restricting market dominance. The European Commission has provided user's rights regarding data portability (to download the user's own data stored on a certain platform and transfer it to another company's platform) in the General Data Protection Regulation (GDPR). With regards to data portability, making it as an obligation to those enterprises possessing market dominance, or making it as a general obligation to all enterprises will result in significantly different effect on competition. This depends on interpretation and application. In the case of a general obligation to all enterprises, discussion on this matter should be carried out with caution because there is a risk that dominant enterprises will become even bigger. Preparation of a global criterion regarding data ownership and portability is also necessary. Either way, it is important to make consumers able to gain access to the information about data collection and utilisation, and to choose enterprises that will use their data appropriately by themselves. It is also important to let the consumers understand the value of their own data better. If the consumers understand the value, their demands towards enterprises that collect the data will be stronger, and the exercise of market dominance may be limited to

[27] *Facebook/Whatsapp* (Case COMP/M.7217) Commission Decision 2014/C 297/04 [2014] OJ C297/13.

a certain extent. The ownership of the data is obscure without a specific solution. There are concern about the possibility that the more data portability is promoted, the less incentive enterprises will be to innovate, or small enterprises' ingenuity of data management will be interrupted. So the discussion should be cautious.

In the future, some obligations of data portability might be imposed on private enterprises even in Japan. Apart from the concern about outflow of data collected with the burden of cost, it is assumed that, the burden of user correspondence and system development and utilisation will become more substantial if obligations are imposed. Although it is very likely that such kind of rules will be imposed only on large-scale enterprises, it is extremely important to draw the line between enterprises that are obligated and those that are not.

5 Future Challenges

Based on people's use of electronic commerce, search engine and communication site, massive data (purchase history, web browsing history, communication history and moving history etc.) are stored on the enterprises' hard disks and clouds. The IT technologies that are used in monitoring the status of machines and devices from aircraft engines with sensors on them and turbines in the wind power stations make massive data obtainable for enterprises. AI technology can analyze such big data, provide better products, services and information to the consumers, and can show its power even in the maintenance work like conserving and replacing parts of a device. Not only in the traditional manufacturing industries, but also in service industries like finance, medicine and nursing, it is expected that such technologies can be widely utilised. However, there are also challenges.

First, together with the acceleration of ICT intelligentisation and data accumulation, development of products and services utilizing the data collected, analyzed, generated and accumulated by the intelligent ICT will not be exclusive to a single enterprise in the future, and new entries will increase, which support an innovation. When data is accumulated and enclosed, under what circumstances should the accumulated data be accessible and disclosed? That criterion (criterion of disclosure) should be clear. In the future, as importance will be attached to the application of data, ventures that give up finding solutions independently and own the technology and data which potentially should have been analyzed by themselves, might be purchased by big enterprises or foreign capitals.

Second, in order to improve research and development capabilities, IT enterprises are trying to purchase companies that have excellent researchers on AI and IoT. The market dominance of those companies is shown not only in the IP rights they hold, but also in the abilities of those excellent people. However, the method to convert that kind of abilities into indicators of market dominance is yet to be developed.

Third, to develop and utilise AI and IoT technologies with specific usage like automatic driving of vehicles and the action of nursing care robots, cooperation among multiple enterprises owning the technologies is necessary. Technology standardisation[28] that acts as a platform for development will probably be established. Therefrom, the standard essential patent (SEP) discharges, and by making the FRAND commitment (condition of license), license negotiation begins with the expectation that the patent technology can be implemented. At that time, if the one who owns the standard essential patent encumbered with FRAND commitment (patent essential to implement specifications), refuses to license or files a lawsuit seeking injunction against the one who has the intention to accept the license under the FRAND terms,[29] and if his act in general makes it difficult to develop, produce and sell the product that adopts the widely spread specifications, thus substantially restricts competition in the specific market, there are cases where his act will fall under the Antimonopoly Act (private monopolisation and unfair trade practices).[30]

Last, the commonisation of API (Application Programming Interface: specification of the interface used in the interchange of software components with each other) has great significance to the success of AI networking. In the field of finance, API is used in the so-called FinTech industry. Obviously, although massive data exists in the information held by banks or credit card companies, such kind of data has not been open so far. On the contrary, banks have the obligation to protect customers' secrets, so there were circumstances where the data could not be really disclosed even to the customers themselves. However, in foreign countries, open API that publishes the connection specification of bank system is developing. In order to improve the settlement service of the bank, especially to encourage non-banks and players to provide more convenient services by using the settlement system of the bank as a platform, even in Japan, financial institutions, IT companies, and the finance administrative authorities being able to participate, the appropriate role of open API has been under discussion from a security perspective in the Financial Services Agency and the Japanese Bankers Association since 2016.

Although FinTech is not addressed in this chapter, one of the challenges of open API originates from the difference of competition environment. To illustrate, if data disclosure is beneficial to the users with a sufficient competition environment, enterprises should have incentives to disclose information in a proper format in order to ensure their competitive advantages. However, in an industry with strong entry regulations, it is hard for such incentives to function. Also, security is very important.

---

[28] The standard here refers to what is established by mutual agreement, in order to be used commonly and repeatedly, in the form of rules concerning activities or the result of the activities, guideline, or document that provides the characteristics, for the purpose of achieving an order that is most suitable for a given situation, and is approved by generally recognized organisations.

[29] Whether it is someone who has the intention to accept the license on FRAND terms or not, is judged based on individual case according to the corresponding situations of both the parties of the license negotiation (for example, whether the fact and the state of infringement of specific standard essential patent are presented, whether the license condition and its reasonable basis are presented, response to the reasonable counter proposal against the presentation, whether the correspondence is honest according to the commercial usage).

[30] Japan Fair Trade Commission, *Guidelines for the Use of Intellectual Property under the Antimonopoly Act* (Tentative translation, 2016). http://www.jftc.go.jp/en/pressreleases/yearly-2016/January/160121.files/IPGL_Frand_attachment.pdf. Accessed 20 December 2017.

The argument of disclosure is difficult because there are severe security requirements when the information being handled is sensitive. Finally, significance of standardisation is essential as it provides cooperating players with convergence way and procedure to connect. In any case, it is necessary to correspond to the failure in a certain sort of market. The necessity of intervention from the government that makes data portability an obligation should also be examined, and industry standardisation of the API in the industrial world should also be requested. At that time, from the perspective of the cost burden of an enterprise, it is reasonable to put certain prerequisites[31] in data disclosure.

6 Summary

This chapter develops a basic analytical framework for ICT infrastructure technology collaboration, focusing on how data and the Internet are linked, with particular attention to the competition stimulated by the prospect of "AI networking". The chapter looks at how AI networking and the competitive ecosystem interact with each other. In this regard, traditional competition theories have difficulty adequately explaining the competition that arises between different layers of ICT networks, which can have a negative impact on disruptive innovation and new value creation. While cooperation is essential for the advancement of AI networks, competition is even more important. It is thus a question of how to balance coordination and competition, which in the context of competition law is a bipolar concept. With respect to the anticompetitive effects resulting from network effects, oligopolistic and monopolistic behavior in AI platforms may occur. In addition, the outputs and programs of AI systems may be modified by learning from the acquired data, creating difficulties in understanding, validating, and controlling the system. It remains unclear how to accurately assess the importance of the data from a competition law perspective. An analysis of the value of this data is recommended. In the context of data accumulation and use, we focused on six topics: market dominance, market definition, abuse of dominance, merger review, personal data protection and competition policy, data ownership and data portability.

References

Collyer K, Mullan H, Timan N (2017) Measuring market power in multi-sided markets. Summer CPI Antitrust Chronicle 1(3):8. www.competitionpolicyinternational.com/wp-content/uploads/2017/09/CPI-Collyer-Mullan-Timan.pdf. Accessed 21 Dec 2017

[31] For example, limiting the connection requests to the quest of the enterprise whose security has been ensured, to the online request with good scalability, and to the important data that is to ensure users' rights.

Ezrachi A, Stucke ME (2015) The curious case of competition and quality. J Antitrust Enforcement 3:227
Graef I (2016) EU competition law, data protection and online platforms: data as essential facility. Wolters Kluwer
Harbour PJ (2007) Dissenting statement of commissioner Pamela Jones Harbour—in the matter of Google/Doubleclick F.T.C. File No. 071-0170. Federal Trade Commission, p 4. www.ftc.gov/sites/default/files/documents/public_statements/statement-matter-google/doubleclick/071220harbour_0.pdf. Accessed 10 Jan 2018
Newman JM (2016) Antitrust in zero-price markets: applications. Wash U L Rev 49 94:64–69
Stucke ME, Grunes AP (2016) Big data and competition policy. OUP

Chapter 4
Competition Law in Digital Age

1 IoT, Big Data, AI, and Antitrust Law

Information and communication technology (ICT) is evolving at an accelerating pace. In 2045 the computer's processing ability is expected to exceed that of humans, reaching a transition where the leading role in technological development and evolution shifts from human to computer. Also, due to the advances in various sensing technologies, including the Internet of Things (IoT) and human information connections, an ever-extending (if not infinite) variety of information is being collected and used. We have already begun to benefit from these technologies through big data, artificial intelligence (AI), robotics, and more. However, these are only the beginnings. A world that has been considered science fiction may be opening to us now and in the next few decades, perhaps in twenty years, with the dramatic progress of AI.

Japan has recently moved to deal with both the upsides and downsides of many developments:

(a) Innovation in IoT has attracted attention in various industries, including manufacturing via the Internet. In IoT, not only humans, but things as well, are targets connected to the Internet, and this connection is expected to create new value. The Japan Fair Trade Commission (JFTC) initiated a Data and Competition Policy Study Meeting to analyze trends in industrial data (including big data), and this effort resulted in the Study Group on Competition Policy Toward the Fourth Industrial Revolution, formed in June 2017 by the Ministry of Economy, Trade, and Industry (METI).

(b) In October 2016, the Ministry of Internal Affairs and the Communication Policy and Information Policy Research Institute convened the AI Network Society Promotion Council to study the social, economic, ethical, and legal issues surrounding AI networking. The council has produced an important report, "Promotion of the Utilization of Report 2018—AI and toward the sound progress of

S. Hayashi and K. Arai, *Digitalization and Competition Policy in Japan*,
https://doi.org/10.1007/978-981-99-5310-3_4

AI networking." Issues relating to big data, AI, antitrust law, and competition policy are now among the hottest topics.

(c) In November 2018, the Japanese government established a study group comprising academics and experts with knowledge of competition policy, information policy, and consumer policy. This group has studied issues and countermeasures surrounding platformers, and culminated in publishing its interim discussion draft (see Sect. 3).

In regard to downsides, first of all, new problems that had not previously been viewed as problems have arisen with the spread of IoT. One problem is the understanding and reaction of companies and users to IoT's specific services. So far, the mainstream thought is to grasp the outcome of IoT from the supply side—that is, from a technological point of view. From now on, however, emphasis will be put on the demand side—that is, what kind of service will bring value to users, including individuals and companies. It is, therefore, necessary to investigate what kind of policy response enhances the value of IoT and contributes to society. We must also respond to risks of IoT, which uses various sensitive and personal data. In addition to direct risks, such as infringement of intellectual property rights and theft of information, this may increase the security risk of enterprises and institutional correspondence. It is necessary to consider privacy concerns of individuals who are the providers of big data.

Big data is an enormous collection of personal information, and its use entails privacy protection problems. Viewpoints are divided among the national government and related institutions whether to deal with big data under competition policy (antitrust law) or consumer protection policy. However, both are needed; for example, the authorities who review business combinations under the Antimonopoly Act should deepen their understanding of the forms of privacy violations in data-driven business and strive to identify anticompetitive factors of such violations.

Privacy infringement of personal information is in the purview of the My Number Act and the Act on the Protection of Personal Information, and is not directly a matter of antitrust law. However, various industries collect data, such as purchase history, web browsing history, communication history, and movement history. Businesses collect this information in the course of their own business activities, and use it to improve their operations. It is sometimes sold to businesses as intellectual property. The buyers may be seeking market dominance through privacy infringement in handling big data, including personal information involved in the integration and acquisition of companies as operating assets. It may be an unfair competition issue that marketing violating privacy is conducted through the collection and process of a large amount of data, and based on which market power is maintained or strengthened. However, it is necessary to keep in mind that the use of privacy data for marketing alone does not cause the problem of antitrust immediately even if the problem of privacy protection arises. It is problematic to use antitrust law to defend against such unfair competition.

Concerning AI, automation has been advancing in recent years together with the progress in AI and ICT. It is expected that new value will be created, and the beginning of advanced services using AI In automatic driving reflects the prospects for such automation. In this regard, the Strategic Headquarters for Promotion of Advanced Information and Telecommunications Network Society, in its meeting of June 15, 2018, adopted the "Public and Private ITS Initiative Road Map 2018". This plan outlines measures to achieve fully automated driving, to promote automatic driving, and thus to make AI gradually more sophisticated.

Scholars of AI predict that, as stated above, AI will outstrip human intelligence in the first half of this century. This phenomenon could open the door to hard-to-detect strategies to eliminate competitors, such as bid rigging with AI or clever skirting of regulations through AI data analysis of large breach cases.

2 What Are the Current Issues?

The progress of ICT brings tremendous changes to the regulation of antitrust law (competition law) governing both large and traditional industries. There are three main issues which have emerged. These issues are discussed below.

2.1 Market Dominance: What Dominates the Market? (Key Concepts of Market Dominance Under the Antimonopoly Act)

Market power is the ability to set a price above the competitive level. The term also refers to power that artificially influences the conditions of transactions. The factors to determine market power over data are quality and quantity of information. These are factors in strengthening control regardless of whether the enterprise in question holds big data in the market. Data is used to quantitatively measure and evaluate the market power of ownership, especially in zero-price markets where market power is somewhat difficult to measure with existing tools. Also, the collection and use of data improves services and brings benefits to consumers.

The feedback loop of business data and revenue is shown as Fig. 1 below. Offering a price reduction attracts price-sensitive consumers and other loop participants (the paid-service consumers who are part of business strategies to increase market power) (Fig. 1).

The simplest way to obtain data is to acquire a business entity that already has big data or suitable human resources (e.g., excellent researchers). The organization that is large enough to make such an acquisition thereby becomes stronger, and its smaller competitors consequently face a more difficult level of market entry; thus, there is a concern that this may reduce competition substantially.

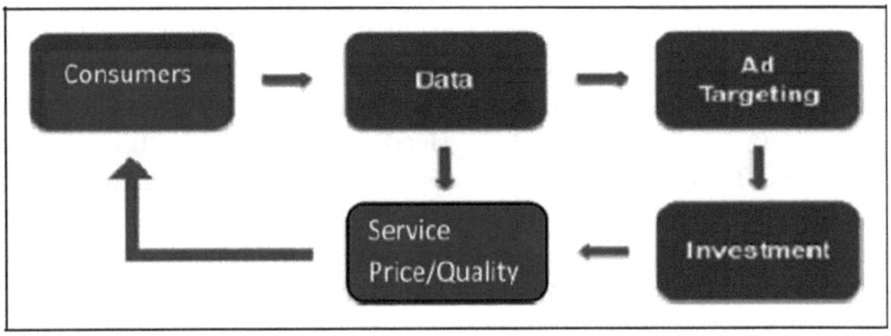

Fig. 1 The feedback loop of business data and revenue

2.2 *How Should Market Dominance Be Measured?*

The study of this issue is called "research and development market research." Currently, we use big data as an indicator of market power. Regarding the measurement method, there is still no exact answer, and this is still on the way to development. However, big data may not necessarily directly link to market dominance. Main features of big data are as follows: (1) non-exclusivity; (2) substitution; (3) timeliness; (4) competition, not only for quantity but also for quality, analysis, and usefulness; and (5) risk of forming entry barriers.

These five pillars all influence competitiveness within the market in some way. Based on data characteristics, anticompetitiveness occurs in collecting or using data. Obtaining data is somewhat essential to businesses, especially in terms of their products and services. Data, especially purchasing behavior data, is an important weapon in marketing. When the source of market power was the market share only, those with strong market positions might have been able to freely control sales prices by limiting sales volume. Those who have a large amount of data on purchasing behavior may be able to freely influence selling prices and excess earnings by devising sales strategies. If a business collects a certain amount of data, it may have more market power, resulting in anticompetitive issues. However, we need to consider anticompetitive harm strictly on a case-by-case basis, particularly in the cases of (a) contracts subject to exclusive restrictions, (b) existence of large enterprises where new entrants face difficulty in obtaining data, and (c) a two-sided market.

Concerning the risk of entry barriers, data is an essential factor for business entities to be competitive in the market. Whether new entrants can compete with existing companies depends upon the nature of the market and innovation. For instance, Microsoft, a company with market dominance in the information technology (IT) industry, was challenged tremendously by Facebook and Google to retain its position. This phenomenon also occurs in oil, steel, and electricity markets. As a result, it is difficult to determine whether business entities in the digital platform, that have the collection of cloud-based software and services businesses' utilities, have sustainable market power under the antitrust law. It is also difficult to use market share as a measurement method. Regarding the digital economy, whether quantitative data (frequency of access to communication sites, usage time, etc.) can be used as a measurement instead of price is also a controversial issue.

Big data forms a complex ecosystem involving multiple products, services, and business operators. Hence, it is difficult to define the market. As a quantitative measurement tool, the Small but Significant and Non-transitory Decline in Quality (SSNDQ) test focusing on quality can be considered instead of the Small but Significant and Non-transitory Increase in Price (SSNIP) test focusing on price. However, it is difficult to apply the SSNDQ test practically; for its application, it is necessary to define quality in an objective, and widely accepted way.

2.3 Abuse of Market Power (Competition Elimination) and AI Cartel (Competition Avoidance)

Acts that abuse market power related to data include: (a) restricting a competitor's access to important data, (b) making it impossible to share or migrate data, and (c) holding data. Regarding such abuse, there is an opinion that "essential facilities doctrine" should be applied. However, it is practically very difficult to prove that data is "essential". In addition, applying "indispensable theory", refusal of business entities possessing data to let others access the data without any justifiable reason is illegal under competition law and is also viewed as abuse of a dominant position.

Apart from abuse of market power, another type of anticompetitive behavior is also widely discussed as business entities use autonomous AI pricing algorithms, called robo-sellers, to set prices in order to optimize profits. This practice unavoidably has the same effect as cartel collusion and inevitably generates a new threat of the price fixing. The authors think that the business entity possessing and using a robo-seller generally is responsible for the result.

3 Government Policy Discussion

Given these circumstances, the Japanese government established a study group comprising academics and experts with knowledge of competition policy, information policy, consumer policy, etc., under the auspices of the METI, the JFTC, and the Ministry of Internal Affairs and Communications (MIC). This group has studied issues and countermeasures surrounding platformers, i.e., the service providers that make up the digital platform. It organized its findings and on November 5, 2018, made public its interim discussion draft.

With regards to this interim draft, the group will conduct business interviews and public comments in the future and will continue to formulate basic principles and implement concrete measures at relevant ministries and agencies such as the METI, the JFTC, and the MIC. The main points of concern are as follows.

1. Significance and characteristics of digital platformers;
2. Legal evaluation perspective on digital platformers;
3. Design of responsibility as leaders of innovation (by way of business law, etc.);
4. Realization of transparency to ensure fairness;
5. Redefinition of fair and free competition;
6. Examination of data transfer/disclosure rules; and
7. International perspective.

The approach outlined above is very comprehensive, and studies are being conducted from various perspectives. Here we briefly explain the seven points itemized above.

First is the significance and characteristics of digital platformers. There are various services, such as online shopping malls, application markets, search services, and social networking services (SNSs), provided on the digital platform. It is considered that these services increase operators' access to the market and improve consumers' benefits. It is said that the digital platform is susceptible to monopolization and oligopoly through characteristics such as network effect, low marginal cost, and economies of scale.

Second, from the viewpoint of legal assessment of digital platformers, it has long been a strong assumption in Japan that they are not actively responsible because they are simply providers (vectors) of places. In recent years, however, there has been a movement to establish certain internet disciplines globally. The discussion draft accordingly proposes that, from the viewpoint of user safety management and consumer protection (when considering business law), domination of digital platformers is the control point of regulation (that is, it is subject to regulation to effectively enforce government rules). With a view to securing the fairness and transparency of digital platforms, a search engine platformer may assume an obligation of disclosing information such as the main parameters to be used and the conditions for access to the data on its platform. The issue should be discussed as to whether it is necessary to examine how to improve the trading environment, based on the following features of very large digital platformers:

1. Digital platformers provide an essential foundation for the social economy.
2. Design, operation, and management of the market itself entails participation of a large number of consumers (data providers) and business operators (data receivers).
3. The use of algorithms to attain market power results in high operability, which causes technical uncertainty.

Third, with regard to the design of responsibility to be a key player in innovation, the draft discusses whether existing business law is appropriate for running a platform business or not. The draft points out the possibility that the existing law cannot exert much control and raises the following issues:

1. Whether the existing business law can exercise appropriate regulation from the viewpoint of social profit and protection of value;
2. Whether making the digital platformer a certain control point can effectively achieve consumer protection and security;
3. Whether equivalence of competition conditions can be secured between existing and new businesses, and between domestic and overseas businesses; and
4. Whether systems can be designed to effectively use certification and auditing methods to secure trust.

From the viewpoint of whether to introduce flexible joint regulation methods, it is necessary to review the business laws in industries that were not necessarily supposed to emerge as platform businesses.

In regards to the fourth point of concern, the realization of transparency for securing fairness, it is unclear how actual transactions surrounding the digital platformer and its users, i.e., business operators and consumers (individuals), are unfair trade practices. This topic is liable to be a hotbed of controversy, and as a starting point for discussing it, a thorough and extensive survey should be conducted to examine issues such as:

1. Whether to use the general investigative power (compulsory investigation authority) granted under Article 40 of the Antimonopoly Act, or to establish a special organization with a certain continuity, to support the law enforcement and policy planning of each ministry;
2. Whether, in the case of establishing such a special organization, to staff it with experts in fields such as law, economics, information processing, system engineering, etc.;
3. How to set design and operation rules for digital platformers;
4. How to continuously investigate and analyze the way platform services are managed;
5. Whether we should also provide legislative recommendations and information to regulatory authorities as a supplement to the Antimonopoly Act; and
6. Whether it is necessary to disclose or specify important transactional conditions, such as introduction of discipline in transactional practices, etc.

As for the fifth point, the redefinition of fair and free competition in the digital market, the platformer provides the essential socioeconomic foundation (i.e., designing and managing the market) and the uncertainty, such as the need to analyze (profile) using algorithms. Yet the platformer's impact may extend further, as in the case of the platformer that is expanding its business to offline fields such as manufacturing. Thus, the impact of a platformer's action on competition is not only online, but also includes offline competitors, and their interrelationship should be considered. Issues are, for example,

1. How do you evaluate the influence of network effect and data accumulation, etc., on the competition in a multi-sided market?
2. How do you think about business combinations in a way that platformers cause potential competitors' harm?
3. In relation to consumers who continue to provide data that is considered to have economic value, do decision makers need to think about applying the regulation of abuse of a superior bargaining position?
4. Is it necessary to consider the tactics of the system, such as the surcharge for appropriate enforcement for deterring violations?

Sixth, regarding data transfer and disclosure, rules such as data portability and application program interface (API) disclosure should be considered not only for consumer policies in data-driven society, but also as a means to improve competition policy and competitive infrastructure. It is essential to consider the necessity of each rule and its contents. It is encouraging that that related mechanisms are also being constructed in the European Union, via its General Data Protection Regulation (GDPR), and in the United States to regulate individuals' electronic access to certain personal data.

Seventh, from an international point of view and considering the fact that platformers are engaged in global activities, it is necessary for international harmony to be concerned about the discipline of digital platformers. It is also essential to consider how to enforce laws and regulations on foreign business operators. However, it is undeniable that there is a point that they are the consideration for regulation since these are mainly the regulatory authorities' efforts by the government. For example, although there is a movement to establish discipline globally in the viewpoint of legal evaluation, it is remarkable that the current movement in the United States is to remove rather than to enforce regulations. It goes without saying that it is faster to respond to global economic movements than to international regulatory trends.

4 Critical Review

The current recognitions and recommendations of the report are comprehensive and based on the latest situation after compliance with the basic principles of economics. However, several points need to be considered carefully from the viewpoints of law and economics. In other words, it is a problem of securing transaction costs, leaders' responsibilities and fairness, as described below.

User safety management and consumer protection are critical issues in terms of transaction costs. In principle, from the perspective of law and economics, if the problem does not affect third parties (no externalities), it is efficient to solve it with a negotiation between the parties and leave it to the justice system. If transaction costs are low, the government does not have to impose any rules. The reduction in transaction cost is the influence of the progress of IT and digitalization, and the level of regulation should be gradually lowered in accordance with the progress of IT.

The responsibilities of the Innovation Leader can be understood emotionally, but it goes without saying that in principle it is economically excessive. If the platform business cannot be regulated by the business law regulating the existing industry, new rules may be not necessary. Imposing further responsibility for such platforms is considered to seek equality of results rather than opportunity equality.

Regulation from the viewpoint of ensuring fairness of transaction is difficult. Those involved in the transaction are considered to be unnecessary to trade if there is no profit obtained from the transaction. From the intervention to the outcome of the transaction, there is certainly the possibility that the government will transfer the profits of the transaction from one party to the other as a distribution policy. However, if this intervention does not explicitly indicate that it is based on a distribution policy, it is possible that policy transparency will be achieved.

There is no need to redefine fair and free competition. In principle, it is possible to tackle the relevant issues with the current competition law system. It is clearly not successful to introduce government-led competition to promote fair competition. It is impossible to introduce competition by means of investing money. Therefore, it is unnecessary to update the competition law itself in response to digitalization, unlike what is happening in the EU and the United States.

Regarding data transfer related rules, in principle, market stakeholders and other stakeholders should respond by themselves. It is not preferable for the government to handle it on a case by case basis. Intervention in data transfer is not stipulated in Japan's competition law (the subcontracting law may be one of its solutions). There are some arguments quoting specific US and/or EU regulations, but the purpose and situation of the law are different, and the government is not supposed to rush to introduce the rules, which are regarded as a way of intervention.

The international viewpoint asserted in the report is considered important. International harmonization and cooperative efforts among authorities need to be appropriately promoted. In this respect, the report is excellent. Indeed, the main purpose of globalization of enterprises is to find the most advantageous areas for business execution. However, as circumstances vary from country to country, if problems arise, national authorities need to strengthen cooperation.

The most inappropriate point of the report is where empirical analysis is not conducted anywhere. Discussions that do not rely on empirical analysis based on econometrics are words with fluffy discussions. Empirical analysis should be carried out in multiple countries.

5 Conclusions

Competition law and policy aim at securing an active competition process in the market to protect customers in their own countries regardless of the nationality of the actors. Hence, Japanese companies controlling overseas platforms are also governed by competition law and policy to ensure the protection of consumers located in their own countries. For example, Japanese companies are making effective use of the services of overseas platform operators or Japanese companies holding industrial data overseas who gain competitive advantage. Regarding data and algorithms of AI, it is necessary to carefully consider the obligation to disclose private enterprises who gather such data through their own investment and ingenuity.

As the platforms become more oligopolistic, the Japanese government has established a data portability rule that enables users to transfer from any specific platform at any time, to open up an environment where new platform-type businesses are created one after another and where active competition is carried out. Features include open APIs that can be connected; development of a fair, free, and transparent competitive environment, including small and medium enterprises and ventures; deregulation to relieve innovation (such as relaxation of entry requirements); social responsibility of digital platformer companies, ensuring fairness to users; and prompt execution of concrete measures in line with this basic principle.

In this policy discussion, it is necessary to seek methods that include realistic international cooperation that is not subject to regulation or intervention-oriented measures. In addition, discussion based on economic empirical analysis is particularly needed. From the viewpoints of ensuring innovative R&D concerning AI and fair competition, in general, the way of the Governance of AI Networking should be a non-regulatory and non-binding way taking technical features and responsibility in distribution among stakeholders (developers, providers, end-users and third parties) into account.

6 Summary

Information and communication technology (ICT) is evolving at an accelerating pace. Competition law and policy aim to secure an active competition process in the market in order to protect customers in their own countries, regardless of the nationality of the actors, including the ICT industry. As the platforms become more oligopolistic, the Japanese government has established a data portability rule that enables users to transfer from any specific platform, at any time, to open up an environment where new platform-type businesses are created one after another and where active competition is carried out. In this policy discussion, it is necessary to seek methods that include realistic international cooperation that is not subject to regulation or intervention-oriented measures. In addition, discussion based on economic empirical analysis is particularly needed. From the viewpoints of ensuring innovative research and development (R&D) concerning artificial intelligence (AI) and fair competition generally, the way of the Governance of AI Networking should be a non-regulatory and anon-binding way, taking technical features and responsibility distribution among stakeholders (developers, providers, end-users and third parties) into account.

Chapter 5
Perspectives on High-Tech Regulation

1 Introduction

Countries around the world, including Japan, are discussing the basic rules for digital markets. For example, recently, on February 18, 2020, the Japanese Cabinet approved the Draft Law on Improving Transparency and Fairness of Particular Digital Platforms. Such rules are intended to ensure fair, transparent trading practices in the rapidly-changing global digital marketplace. These rules also aim to promote the digitalization of society to facilitate further economic growth and increased productivity. To this end, various measures are being taken to promote data distribution and private-sector digital reform/revolution, with the overarching goal of fostering an advanced communications environment suitable for the fifth-generation era.

Responses from the society and the market demonstrate recognition of the need for digital market rules. However, consideration should be given to whether an undue burden is being imposed on the platform side and whether there is general reluctance on the consumer side.

Regarding the public's perception of intelligent machines and systems as a core component of the digital market, public opinion has shown strong support for the production of so-called public goods as well as the active introduction of artificial intelligence (AI) in areas where human intellectual labor is costly (Arai 2018). In other words, this result means that the public is aware that any task that is substantially beneficial should be done by humans. It has also been shown that investigating the need to adopt AI in a given situation is equivalent to investigating the public's perception of the difficulty of that situation.

An analysis based on survey data that polled people's attitudes toward artificial AI speakers, which comprise one of the most familiar media representing intelligent machines and systems, shows that people who are already using this form of AI or are socially dominant are more willing to use AI speakers (My Voice 2018, 2019). In the context of modern society, it is strongly suggested that people's awareness of intelligent machines and systems is dependent on their sensitivity to information. In other words, people who are sensitive to information-gathering are more proactive

S. Hayashi and K. Arai, *Digitalization and Competition Policy in Japan*,
https://doi.org/10.1007/978-981-99-5310-3_5

in terms of acquiring information, while those who are not are more reluctant to access information. Although only a limited number of people are inclined to invest in expensive AI speakers, they tend to make such an investment when it is necessary. The analysis also finds that online shopping is more prevalent among those who are below a certain age, command incomes above a certain level, and have limited daytime consumption opportunities due to their work (Cabinet Office 2018).

Those who are skilled in obtaining information tend to have superior information-processing abilities, while those who are not skilled in handling information tend to be left behind. As a result, disparities may arise and existing gaps may widen. With the rise of the platform business, it has been repeatedly pointed out that the profitability of information processing and information analysis, especially AI, may increase. It also points to economies of scale. In light of this, it is important to pay attention to the importance of providing appropriate alternatives and maintaining competition when introducing AI and other intelligent machines and systems into society. In this case, the platform's market dominance could be one of several points of contention. On the other hand, in this regard, it is not clear whether the basic rules of the digital market should be determined by the interventionism approach, if a natural monopoly constitutes the only difference in terms of characteristics (economies of scale) between the present and the previous/traditional goods. However, even if such characteristics are taken into account, rules for promoting initial investment and demand are considered necessary in order to ensure a basis for competition.

Meanwhile, the public sector is attempting to improve the transparency and fairness of AI's introduction into society. As a symbol of the Japanese government's recent digital market regulation strategy, the following governmental measures and actions have been taken to ensure transparency and fairness:

(i) By creating 'a bill on improving transparency of transactions of digital platform operators' (provisional name) to ensure transparency in digital platform transactions, the government and the public sector are seeking to overarchingly improve the transparency and fairness of digital platforms, which are multi-sided markets with a network effect, while also improving disclosure, procedures, and systems for providing services over the Internet (to those who frequently use online malls and/or app stores) in order to protect trading partners. This has a significant impact on people's lives and the national economy.

(ii) Following a review of the Act on the Protection of Personal Information, rules shall be made to strengthen the individual's role in the collection and use of personal data, improve the convenience aspect of personal data, mandate personal notification when there are leaks, etc., and develop mechanisms to promote voluntary rules for business operators, etc., since business operators need to be held accountable for their responsibilities.

(iii) Improvements in antitrust rules, including the evaluation of the value of data are also being promoted, along with improvements pertaining to the idea of certain trading areas, taking the multi-sided market into account through the revision of business combination guidelines, and improvements pertaining to the idea of substantive limits/restricts on competition, taking network effects into account.

(iv) To combat digital platform operators' abuse of their dominant position in relation to consumers, rules are being made to clarify how such abuse operates in the company–consumer relationship.

(v) Regarding the assessment of the competitive situation in the digital advertising market, a related company is striving, in line with government instructions, to improve the transparency of the measures that are being taken to address concerns about profiling based on the acquisition of personal data.

These measures can be interpreted as clarifying the government's basic stance and focusing on ensuring a competitive base. However, rules aimed at creating alternative, complementary means of digital platform regulation are insufficient, and regulations are on the verge of being implemented, which is an approach that is generally categorized as interventional. For this reason, there is a need to plan based on research and surveys, on the premise that national industrial and competition authorities act to promote competition.

The government has had a longstanding interest in preventing market failure and promoting innovation in strategic industries. Public policy on domestic technology is critical to both national security and economic prosperity, hence the network governance that is often used in public administration has been analyzed (Whetsell et al. 2020). Governments often seek to boost their international competitiveness by promoting private-sector cooperative activities at the inter-organizational level, and indeed, this has been attempted. However, while research on network governance has examined the regulation of market power, evaluating that regulation remains a challenge for the administration. We have been working on the following issues; with respect to the study's status so far, we have discussed network governance (Klijn and Koppenjan 2015; Provan and Kenis 2008) and social network analysis (Lubell et al. 2012; Lusher et al. 2013). In addition, for example, Andrews et al. (2011) studied public and organizational performance, and Meier and O'Toole (2011) found an impact on the management of public and private organizations. However, how public administration should regulate industrial organization and market dominance remains a challenge. In particular, the question of how to regulate digital platforms in the context of increasingly sophisticated science and technology is a major issue that needs to be studied at this time. In particular, today, online intermediaries, as gatekeepers of information, have become the primary target of various policy and legislative measures, and the area of their rights and obligations is being debated (Montagnani and Trapova).

In this chapter, this gap is bridged by the tradition of constitutional theory and other traditions against efforts to achieve market dominance. We propose a new theoretical methodology that uses a new theoretical approach, which is applied to actual digital platform regulations and evaluated. Present-day public administration is in need of such an evaluation method. Such an evaluation methodology is needed today in public administration as well. Furthermore, the limitation here is that theoretical considerations (the presentation of the study's methodology) constitute the study's main focus.

This chapter is aimed at general theoretical applications by taking out the Japanese material and making it of general theoretical application. Based on the theoretical methodology presented in this chapter, an assessment of the Japanese regulatory system is conducted, and through doing so, the theory is put into practice.

When developing and enforcing basic rules, consideration should be given not only to the clarity and predictability of rules and regulations in business activities, but also to investment in basic research and its practical applications. This is supported by the fact that the owners of intelligent machines and systems also support the active introduction of AI into so-called public goods, and those who decide to invest in the introduction of AI into everyday life tend to increase their investments in other areas (Arai 2018). Therefore, it is considered essential to improve consumer awareness and the diffusion of intelligent machines and systems in society.

In the next section, this chapter identifies problems in the current industrial organization. In this context, the chapter also deals with the technical issues of competition law. However, the basic question pertains to approaches to market dominance, confronting the primary public administration issue. Section 3 discusses the forthcoming regulation of this salient issue and examines the necessary and sufficient conditions for regulation from a legitimacy perspective. First, it presents the key points to consider when examining the need for regulation from a legitimacy perspective. Second, it delineates the factors to be considered when examining the sufficiency of regulation in terms of legitimacy. Third, it performs an analysis from a causal perspective. Section 3 specifically probes the adequacy of Japan's digital platform regulation from multiple perspectives. Section 4 presents this study's conclusions. In addition, the study's implications and their practical applications are described.

Current Problems

Advances in and the development of information and communication technologies (ICT) will bring about major changes in the regulation of antitrust (competition) law, which governs both large and traditional industries. The following three main issues are discussed:

(i) Market power: what controls the market? (The main concept of market control under antitrust law)
(ii) How do we measure market dominance?
(iii) The abuse of market dominance (the exclusion of competition) and the AI cartel (the avoidance of competition).

2 Market Power

The first issue is market power (the main concept of market control under antitrust law).

Market power is the ability to set prices above a competitive level. It also refers to the power to artificially influence the terms of a transaction. The factors that determine market dominance in data relate to information quality and quantity. These are factors that may or may not lead to greater control of the market, regardless of whether the company in question possesses big data.

Data constitute a somewhat difficult element for measuring market forces, especially with the existing tools. The existing tools that are used to quantitatively measure and evaluate market dominance may be somewhat difficult to apply, especially in free data circulation markets.

In addition, the collection and utilization of data improves services, thus benefitting consumers. There is a feedback loop in business data and revenue. Proposing price reductions attracts price-sensitive consumers and other loop participants (such as consumers of paid services who are part of a business strategy to increase market dominance). The feedback is that further data collection becomes possible.

The easiest way to get data is to acquire entities that already have big data in addition to valuable human resources (e.g., good researchers). Organizations that are large enough to make such acquisitions are more powerful. As a result, smaller competitors face more difficulty entering the market. It is therefore feared that competition will be significantly reduced if this happens.

Measuring Market Dominance

The problem here is very similar to what is called the 'research and development market.' We are now trying to use big data as an indicator of market dominance. However, there is still no precise answer that vouches for this measurement method, and it can be said to still be under development. Big data is not necessarily directly tied to market dominance.

The main characteristics of the data and of data processing are as follows:

(1) non-exclusivity; (2) substitution; (3) timeliness; (4) competition, not only for quantity, but also for quality, analysis, and usefulness; and (5) the risk of creating entry barriers. These five characteristics impact market competitiveness, to some extent.

Based on the characteristics of a particular dataset, a reduction in competition will occur when collecting or using the data. Data capture is essential for companies, especially in terms of products and services. If companies collect a certain amount of data, their market dominance may increase, and competition may decrease.

In light of this reality, it is necessary to examine the lack of competitiveness in the following cases:

(a) contracts subject to monopoly regulation
(b) the presence of large firms that have difficulty obtaining data on new entrants
(c) the two-sided market.

With respect to barriers to entry, data constitute a significant factor (a kind of essential) in firms' marketplace competitiveness. New entrants' ability to compete with incumbent firms is determined by both the nature of the market and innovation. For example, Microsoft is trying to maintain its position as a market-dominant player in the information technology (IT) industry. However, the company was aggressively challenged by Facebook and Google, and this phenomenon has also recently been seen in the oil, steel, and power markets. Businesses on digital platforms are collections of cloud-based software and services. It is difficult to determine whether a person has sustainable market control under antitrust laws.

Using market share as a measurement method is also generally difficult. In the digital economy, there is also a controversial debate as to whether quantitative data (the frequency of access to communication sites, the duration of use, etc.) can assume a measurement role in place of price. It is also controversial whether quantitative data (e.g., frequency of access to communication sites, time of use, etc.) can be used as a measurement rather than a price. Big data creates a complex ecosystem, involving multiple products, services, and operators.

Therefore, defining markets is a difficult task. As a quantitative measurement tool, consideration can be given to small, significant, non-temporary price increases that are focused on small but significant non-transitory increase in price (SSNIP) tests instead of quality-focused, small-scale, significant temporary small but significant non-degradation transitory decrease in quality (SSNDQ). However, it is difficult to apply the SSNDQ test in practice, as it requires an objective, popular definition of 'quality.'

The Abuse of Market Power (Competition Exclusion) and AI Cartels (Competition Avoidance).

The abuse of market power in relation to data can be assumed to include the following:

(a) competitors restricting access to critical data
(b) making it impossible to share or migrate data
(c) enclosing and retaining data.

Some are of the opinion that the 'essential facility doctrine' should be applied to such abuses. There is a United States antitrust theory that an operator whose facilities are essential to market competition may not deny a competitor access to those facilities. However, in practice, it is very difficult to prove that a particular dataset constitutes an 'essential facility.' It is also difficult to establish that prohibiting an operator who owns the data from allowing others to access it without good cause is a refusal based on 'indispensability.'

Apart from the abuse of market dominance, there is another widely-discussed type of anti-competitive behavior in which companies use automated AI pricing algorithms (robo-sellers) to optimize their profits. Such actions inevitably have the same effect as cartel collusion, thus creating new threats. However, with respect to algorithmic collusion, some have pointed out that while improved demand forecasting may facilitate coordination among sellers, it may also increase the temptation for each firm to deviate to a lower price during periods of predicted high demand

(Miklos-Thal and Tucker 2019). For this reason, each situation must be carefully considered, and empirical analyses should be accumulated.

Some argue that, for example, the entity that develops and uses robots is responsible for any resulting matters pertaining to robot development and use; therefore, careful consideration should be given to whether the company developing the algorithm should also be subject to this principle.

3 Discussion

One approach to tackling these problems is to empirically estimate market dominance and uncover the kinds of caveats that are concomitant with ICT advances as well as how these affect the regulation of antitrust (competition) law, which governs both large and traditional industries. Another approach would be a legal theoretical one, with critical discussion of the nature of regulation. Arai and Hayashi (2020) analyzed the former approach to estimate two-sided market power in railway companies. For business operators in multi-sided markets, the indirect network effect does not appear uniformly, and it is therefore important to look at securing appropriate competition on a case-by-case basis. From the perspective of ensuring innovative AI-related research and development (R&D) as well as fair competition, it is generally considered that, taking technical features and the division of responsibilities among stakeholders into account, the governance of AI networking should be non-regulatory and non-binding because multi-sided marketability is assumed and various effects can therefore be expected.

In this chapter, the necessary and sufficient conditions for competition law enforcement are reviewed from the perspective of legitimacy. The circumstances under which competition law enforcement is necessary in the context of ICT development and under which such enforcement is sufficient to achieve the objective are critically examined in the context of rules to ensure transparency in digital platform transactions. This is an attempt to look at the conditions of law enforcement not only in the short term, but also to discuss the necessity and sufficiency of policy responses in the medium to long term.

3.1 Necessary Conditions

The circumstances under which competition law enforcement is required are those where the price is set above the competitive level and the transaction terms are artificially influenced. When data are associated with market dominance, the quality and quantity of information are relevant. When deciding whether market dominance is formed, maintained or strengthened, the question arises as to how to control the market, regardless of whether the company in question possesses big data. In this approach, AI and big data can be powerful tools. For this reason, when making rules toward improving transparency and fairness in digital platform transactions, a competition policy is never unnecessary. In so doing, the central issue is to protect the interests of the providers and the users of goods, as listed in the bill, and in service of that goal, necessary measures such as the disclosure of information like transaction terms and conditions, ensuring fairness in operations, reporting on the status of operations, and publishing the results of evaluations and assessments are being carefully considered, without, to use a metaphor, bending the horns to kill the cattle (or spoiling the ship for a half-penny's worth of tar).

It is also necessary to consider how competition policy will respond positively to developments in digital platform trading that go beyond the need for mere individual legislation. For example, (even) the purpose of the bill is explained with reference to the points of attention in the bill's implementation; that is, 'Based on the voluntary and proactive rules of digital platform providers, the involvement from the State shall be necessarily minimized, and mutual understanding in the business relationship between digital platform providers and users of goods, etc., shall be promoted' (Ministry of Economy, Trade and Industry 2020). It goes without saying that even if these aspects are included in the bill's enactment, how the competition policy will be implemented in practice will depend on the rules for all stakeholders.

When examining the need for digital platform regulation, discussion must begin with the legitimacy of regulation. In this discussion of the constitution's raison d'être, legitimacy is first and foremost a sociological acceptance (moral legitimacy). This is then explained as something that dependent on an inherently uncertain foundation, but is acknowledged by an expectation of the future. Furthermore, it is pointed out that the intertwined relationship between practical urgency and moral legitimacy must be taken into account on many issues that are ostensibly legal in the absence of a larger legal and sociological consensus.

First, in the context of competition policy, the aspect that requires sociological acceptance is the part that requires responding to society's vague anxieties (such as with respect to their transparency and fairness) about new technologies. It can be considered from two sides: negative and positive freedom. In other words, the part of the bill that corresponds to the former brings about negative clearance regarding the policy's legitimacy in the strong sense that public opinion should offer appropriate support, while the part of the bill that corresponds to the latter promotes competition, including new entries into the market, thus regarding legitimacy in the weak sense that public opinions will tolerate.

Second, where moral legitimacy is required, consideration must be given to the assumption that the welfare situation brought about by the competition policy will not be worse in the sense that minimal rather than ideal things are required. In this sense, when examining the bill and its background, more careful consideration should be given to the bill itself or to the idea of introducing direct competition that plays an important role in dramatically improving market access. In other words, it has been theoretically and empirically confirmed that competition does not improve via promotion, but rather by achieving an endogenous competitive situation with minimal response. It goes without saying, then, that subsidies for individual companies and the promotion of industrial policies both need attention. That is, what is important as a rule involves ideal theory as well as minimalist theory, and the minimal moral legitimacy of a rule does not guarantee the minimal moral legitimacy of all actions under that rule (Fallon 2005).

Third, with respect to whether this rule relies on an inherently uncertain foundation, thus allowing for confidence in the future, the inherent uncertainty is acknowledged and positive confidence in digital platforms, including AI and big data, is believed to have been gained.

Therefore, when discussing from the perspective of the legitimacy of the need for regulation, it is important to ensure at least the minimum that is necessary. In addition, with regard to the sufficiency of regulation, this will be a problem that must be solved when discussing the sufficient condition and is, in fact, not solved yet.

3.2 *Sufficient Conditions*

One situation in which competition law enforcement is sufficient is that it is possible to achieve its objectives through rules to improve the transparency and fairness of digital platform transactions in order to prevent the formation, maintenance, and strengthening of market dominance, and this must be verified. Peripheral interventions related to the operations of individual businesses, such as information disclosure, ensuring operational fairness, and reporting on the status of operations, are hardly sufficient enough to be expected to exert an effect on the core parts of the business, such as sales, scale expansion, and R&D. Furthermore, the purpose of regulation is difficult to achieve if these rules merely affect operators' behavior.

This requires not only a legal argument pertaining to the legitimacy of regulatory policies, but also a discussion of legitimacy from the perspectives of political science and social psychology. The issue of legitimacy in policy execution is also being discussed in the context of political science. For example, Weber organizes legitimacy-backed dominance in the following three categories: legal, traditional, and charismatic dominance. The sources of legitimacy can include long-term existence, good governance, governance mechanisms (fair representation and voice), and manipulation through the use of national symbols, which is also in line with Fallon's view. This chapter, however, will not pursue the significance of legitimacy itself; rather, it will take the legitimacy of policy implementation as a perspective.

Furthermore, the elements that constitute legitimacy in policy implementation are analyzed via social psychology's elaboration likelihood model, which explains how people can be persuaded to change their attitudes (Arai 2012). Having been fashioned as an offshoot of the cognitive response approach, this model distinguishes the two processing responses as motivating information processing and recognizing peripheral events, and has also absorbed the heuristic model's findings. In applying these to the legitimacy of policy implementation, 'resources' and 'reflectiveness' are needed from the perspective of motivating content processing with regard to the elements of attitude change in core participants; meanwhile, 'expertise,' 'cognition,' and 'results' are considered to be problematic with regard to the elements of attitude change in peripheral participants because such people do not sufficiently consider the persuasive message on a daily basis, and they judge the message using non-essential peripheral cues around expertise verification and feelings of like and dislike.

However, unlike in the debate on the legitimacy of administrative agencies, the same argument is difficult to make with respect to digital platform regulation. The framework of the discussion itself can be considered motivating content processing because of the reception of the business side of policy implementation or because of peripheral cues as indicators of the reception of peripheral participants and stakeholders. However, the validity of the items that are under consideration should be judged individually, and there are cases in which that indicator has to be qualitative.

With these considerations in mind, this chapter will examine the items one by one with respect to the sufficiency of the rules. In terms of resources, it is hard to say that they are appropriate from the perspective of budgetary personnel, even with digital platform regulation as the tool. In terms of reflection, it is presumed that a certain degree of reflection has been ensured, where actual law enforcement will proceed with the relevant parties' consent. Motivating content processing is considered to involve too many challenges to be a sufficient condition. In addition, in terms of peripheral cues from peripheral participants, perceptions of the aggregate stakeholders' expertise tend to indicate that digital platform operators outperform regulated entities, highlighting the need to determine whether the policy is implementable. With respect to exposure as recognition, it is difficult to assert that certain privacy protection rules are themselves acceptable enough to satisfy the policy's urgency, but they are convincing as far as the cost of doing so is concerned. In terms of results, whether the policy's implementation can be expected to improve convenience and total welfare is questionable, and competition must be ensured on the digital platform side, which is difficult to achieve simply by removing the adverse effects of policy implementation.

Therefore, when discussing the sufficiency of regulation with respect to the element of legitimacy, it is unreasonable to expect effectiveness, especially from peripheral participants, and motivating content processing is also considered to be problematic.

3.3 *Causal Inference*

Furthermore, even if partial policy implementation satisfies the necessary and sufficient conditions, a major question remains as to whether the causal relationship involving the policy objectives can be expected to be achieved. A discussion needs to be held about how policy responses to digital platforms can be positioned within the framework of competition policy as a response to market dominance.

Policy responses to digital platforms can be positioned primarily as part of consumer protection and small and medium-sized enterprise (SME) policy, rather than being understood in a competition policy framework, as we have seen thus far. This has been described and analyzed in terms of freedom of business (freedom of association and freedom of choice of occupation) and the protection of property rights, and it has also been discussed in the context of administrative policy implementation as protecting positive freedom from incursions by negative freedom. However, when administrative policy implementation conflicts with the basic principles of competition policy, there cannot always be a positive evaluation. For example, antitrust thinking about administrative guidance also requires a detailed examination of purpose, content, and method, which is not straightforward with regard to guidance on basic competition variables.

Therefore, if we return to this principle and take measures to ensure the normal functioning of the market mechanism, it should be understood in the framework of competition policy, but because transparency and fairness beyond that are difficult to imagine, various protection policies should be understood in a framework that is separate from the market mechanism. When the two policies conflict, necessity and sufficiency must be grasped from the perspective of legitimacy in order to determine the gains and losses, and intervention with respect to the competition variables should be minimized to evaluate it in the competition policy framework. Furthermore, empirical considerations are needed when formulating actual policies and charters.

For example, Arai and Hayashi (2020) examined two-sided marketability between segments in the rail business, confirming, not only through panel analysis, but also through difference-in-difference analysis, internal subsidies' potential with respect to leisure services and distribution in the transport business as well as the real estate business's indirect network effect. From the perspective of preventing the abuse of market dominance, this information should be better utilized in the future, that is, as part of the background information that needs to be more closely examined in the event of any suspicious activity.

4 Concluding Remarks

Competition law and policy aim to ensure an active competition process in the market to protect the country's customers, regardless of the nationalities of the parties. Therefore, Japanese companies with overseas platforms are subject to competition law and policy in order to ensure the protection of consumers who are located in their home country. For example, locally-based Japanese companies are making effective use of services offered by overseas Japanese companies that are gaining competitive advantages through the possession of industrial data or from overseas platform operators. It is necessary to cautiously consider the disclosure obligations of private companies that collect AI data and algorithms through their own investment and ingenuity.

As the oligopoly of platforms persists, the Japanese government has established data portability rules that allow migration from a particular platform at any time. This has created an environment where new platform-based businesses are born one after another and active competition is taking place. This environmental improvement will include the following:

(i) open APIs that can be connected/are connectable with open application program interfaces (APIs)
(ii) A fair, free, transparent competitive environment for small and medium-sized businesses and ventures
(iii) deregulation to facilitate innovation (e.g., the deregulation of market entry, etc.)
(iv) digital platform companies' social responsibility to ensure user fairness.

Specific measures that are in line with this basic policy must be implemented promptly. Furthermore, this policy discussion should include realistic international cooperation that is not subject to regulatory or interventionist measures. In addition, discussions based on economic empirical analysis are particularly necessary for these studies. In actual policy discussion, it is also necessary to use counterfactuals to further improve the accuracy of the analysis.

In this chapter, digital platform regulation in the context of the development and upgrading of science and technology is discussed from the perspective of legitimacy, especially with regard to the necessary sufficient condition of regulation. The need for regulation means that market dominance is being exercised, or is likely to be exercised, and that previous regulation was insufficient, thus confirming that some action is required. The chapter considered, in terms of legitimacy, first, sociological acceptance, second, moral legitimacy, and third, whether the proposed regulation relies on a foundation of inherent uncertainty but is allowed by virtue of expectations of the future. It is likely that sociology would make allowances for what should be subject to discipline in today's flourishing digital platform (as many recognize). It is also likely that regulation is not the minimum that is necessary for moral legality. There is uncertainty about the future, but there is also an expectation of regulation.

The sufficiency of this regulation explains how persuasion can be effective in changing people's attitudes, specifically as it relates to the elaboration likelihood model of social psychology, which is a 'resource' and 'reflection' model from the perspective of motivation for content processing; 'degree,' 'expertise,' 'cognition,' and 'results' were considered in terms of judging the message using non-essential peripheral cues. While the level of reflection may be adequate, other resource aspects, perceptions of expertise, exposure as recognition, and digital platform results are difficult to achieve through policy implementation. In addition, the causal relationship was also examined, but further empirical analysis was considered to be desirable in this phase. Therefore, the digital platform regulation that has been introduced in Japan is not as effective in terms of necessary and sufficient conditions. It is something that has not been explicitly clarified through the steady execution of the policy that follows at this time of public administration.

The government had an interest in preventing market failure and promoting innovation in strategic industries. In particular, ways of thinking about the regulation of digital platforms in light of increasingly sophisticated science and technology constitute a major issue that needs to be studied imminently. However, because this is a new field, and because the methods of regulation themselves are still being debated, there has not been much public administration evaluation of regulation itself.

In this chapter, this gap is bridged by the tradition of constitutional theory and other traditions against efforts at market dominance. We developed a new theoretical methodology that employs a new theoretical approach, which was applied to actual digital platform regulation and evaluated. Needless to say, such an evaluation methodology is needed in public administration as well. The limitation here is that the theoretical considerations (the presentation of the study's methodology) are this chapter's main focus. It should be noted that a quantitative analysis is needed.

From the perspective of ensuring innovative AI-related R&D and fair competition, it is generally desirable that the governance of AI networking should be non-regulatory and non-binding, taking technical features and divided responsibilities among stakeholders (i.e., developers, providers, end users, and third parties) into account. This is because for business operators in multi-sided markets, the appearance of indirect network effects is not uniform, and it is important to examine the security surrounding appropriate competition on a case-by-case basis.

5 Summary

This chapter examines necessary and sufficient conditions in terms of legitimacy with respect to digital platform regulation in the context of today's development and refinement of sophisticated science and technology. With the increasing oligopoly of platforms, the government has established data portability that allow data to be shifted from a particular platform at any time, creating an environment in which new platform-based businesses can emerge and vigorous competition can take place. In terms of legitimacy, this article considers the following necessary conditions: first, sociological acceptance; second, moral legitimacy; and third, reliance on a foundation that is inherently uncertain but allowable through expectations of the future. As a sufficient condition, the chapter also discusses applying social psychology's elaboration likelihood model, which explains how persuasion is particularly effective in changing people's attitudes. This approach analyzes 'resources' and 'reflectivity' in terms of motivating content processing, and 'expertise,' 'cognition,' and 'consequences' in terms of judging the message based on non-essential peripheral cues. In addition, the point of causality is also examined, and, here, further empirical analysis is needed. In this regard, the digital platform regulation that has been introduced in Japan has not been clarified in terms of necessity and sufficiency.

References

Andrews R, Boyne GA, Walker RM (2011) Dimensions of publicness and organizational performance: a review of the evidence. J Public Adm Res Theory 21(3):i301–i319. https://doi.org/10.1093/jopart/mur026

Arai K (2018) Intelligent machines and systems and awareness of responsibility. Trans Artif Intell Soc 33(3):B-H32_1–7

Arai K (2012) Administrative performance and legitimacy: an elaboration likelihood approach to competition authorities in Japan and the United States. Public Perform Manag Rev 36(1):54–78

Arai K, Hayashi S (2020) AI, big data and competition. In: Annual meeting of Japan economic policy association

Cabinet Office (2018) Annual economic and financial report for fiscal year 2018. https://www5.cao.go.jp/j-j/wp/wp-je18/index_pdf.html

Fallon RH Jr (2005) Legitimacy and the constitution. Harv Law Rev 118(6):1787–1853

Klijn EH, Koppenjan J (2015) Governance networks in the public sector. Routledge

Lubell M, Scholz J, Berardo R, Robins G (2012) Testing policy theory with statistical models of networks. Policy Stud J 40(3):351–374

Lusher D, Koskinen J, Robins G (2013) Exponential random graph models for social networks: theory, methods, and applications. Cambridge University Press, New York

Meier KJ, O'Toole LJ Jr (2011) Comparing public and private management: theoretical expectations. J Public Adm Res Theory 21(3):i283–i299. https://doi.org/10.1093/jopart/mur027

Miklós-Thal J, Tucker C (2019) Collusion by algorithm: does better demand prediction facilitate coordination between sellers? Manage Sci 65(4):1552–1561

Ministry of Economy, Trade and Industry (2020) The purpose of the proposed legislation. https://www.meti.go.jp/press/2019/02/20200218001/20200218001.html

My Voice (2018, 2019) Survey of smart speakers. https://www.myvoice.co.jp/biz/surveys/23507/index.html, https://www.myvoice.co.jp/biz/surveys/24909/index.html

Provan KG, Kenis P (2008) Modes of network governance: structure, management, and effectiveness. J Public Adm Res Theory 18(2):229–252

Whetsell T, Siciliano MD, Witkowski KGK, Leiblein MJ (2020) Government as network catalyst: accelerating self-organization in a strategic industry. J Public Adm Res Theory 30(3):448–464. https://doi.org/10.1093/jopart/muaa002

Part III
The Realities of Various Digital Regulations

Part III of this book examines various factors to consider in the digital realm. It describes a number of perspectives that must be considered when enforcing competition law, including factors involved, areas that require regulation, and the transforming nature of the economy in free business activity.

Chapter 6
Data Regulation

1 Introduction

This chapter provides an introduction and an overview to the international rules for online platform operators,[1] with a focus on EU recent developments and the debate surrounding data transfer and distribution. In Section 2, after an overview of the EU digitalization policy, the EU's regulation on platform-to-business relations and the European Data Strategy are briefly introduced. Next, in Section 3, an introduction and a discussion are given focusing on the status of Japan. Last, in Section 4, a conclusion is drawn to summarize the findings presented in this chapter.

2 Movements in the EU

2.1 Progress of Digitalization Policy Since 2010

The EU's policies for the digitalization of society and the economy could be divided into three periods: the period of reviewing in light of the transition from analogue to digital legislation (Period I, 2010–2014), which is symbolized by the EU policy paper "A Digital Agenda for Europe" (2010), the period of preparing digital legislation/action plans (Period II, 2015–2017), symbolized by "A Digital Single Market Strategy for Europe" (2015), and the period of introducing digital legislation since 2018 (Period III, the period of transposing into national legislation).

[1] Although it is rather common to refer to "online platform operators" as "digital platformers" in Japan, this chapter uses the term "online platform operators" for the reader's convenience. The definition of "online platform" is, in line with the wording provided in the "Act on Enhancing Transparency and Fairness of Specified Digital Platforms" described below, a place established by information processing using a computer with the intention of being used by a large number of persons via the Internet, and goods, services or rights are provided therein.

S. Hayashi and K. Arai, *Digitalization and Competition Policy in Japan*,
https://doi.org/10.1007/978-981-99-5310-3_6

The main EU policy papers, regulations and directives related to the digital market issued during Period I include the Spatial Information Directive in the EC (March 2007)[2], "Open data—An engine of innovation, growth and transparent governance" (December 2011),[3] "Towards better access to scientific information: Boosting the benefits of public investments in research" (July 2012),[4] " Unleashing the Potential of Cloud Computing in Europe" (September 2012),[5] Directive on the reuse of public sector information" (June 2013),[6] "Towards a thriving data driven economy" (July 2014),[7] eIDAS Regulation (Electronic Identification and Trust Services Regulation) (July 2014),[8] etc.

In Period II, "A Digital Single Market Strategy for Europe" (May 2015),[9] Directive on Information Provision Procedures in Technical Rules and Rules for Information Society Services (September 2015),[10] Open Internet Regulation (November 2015),[11] Payment Services Directive 2 (November 2016),[12] "Digitisating European Industry Reaping the full benefits of a Digital Single Market" (April, 2016),[13] European Cloud Initiative (April, 2016),[14] "General Data Protection Regulation" (May 2016),[15] Proposed amendments to the "Audiovisual Media Services Directive" (May 2016),[16] "A comprehensive approach to stimulating cross-border e-Commerce for Europe's citizens and businesses" (May 2016),[17] Directive on the Protection of Trade Secrets (June 2016),[18] Network and Information Security Directive (July 2016),[19] "Building the European Data Economy" (January, 2017),[20] Proposal for a Regulation on Privacy and Electronic Communications (January 2017),[21] Medical Device Regulation (April

[2] Directive 2007/2/EC.

[3] COM (2011) 882.

[4] COM (2012) 401.

[5] COM (2012) 529.

[6] Directive 2013/37/EU.

[7] Com (2014) 442.

[8] Regulation (EU) 910/2014.

[9] COM (2015) 192.

[10] Directive (EU) 2015/1535.

[11] Regulation (EU) 2015/2120. Regarding network neutrality, see, Hayashi (2017).

[12] Directive (EU) 2015/2366 ("PSD2").

[13] COM (2016) 180.

[14] COM (2016) 178.

[15] Regulation (EU) 2016/679 ("GDPR").

[16] COM (2016) 287.

[17] COM (2016) 320. For an analysis of the Unfair Trading Directive and an introduction to the subsequent amendments by the Modernization Directive, see Antonios Karaiskos, Unfair Trading Practices and Private Law Theory: A Comparative Analysis with EU Law (Law Bunka, 2020), p. 107 et seq.

[18] Directive (EU) 2016/943.

[19] Directive (EU) 2016/1148.

[20] COM (2017) 9.

[21] COM (2017) 10.

2017),[22] Summary report of the public consultation on the evaluation of Database Directive (October 2017),[23] etc., were published.

In Period III, Geo-blocking Regulation (February 2018),[24] Online Illegal Content Recommendation (March 2018),[25] "Tackling online disinformation: a European Approach" (April 2018),[26] "EU Code of Practice on Disinformation" (October 2018),[27] Proposal for a Regulation on a framework for the free flow of non-personal data in the European Union (November 2018),[28] European Electronic Communications Code (December 2018),[29] Digital Content Directive (May 2019),[30] Sale of Goods Directive (May 2019),[31] Open Data Directive (June 2019),[32] Online Intermediation Services Regulation (July 2019),[33] "Model Rules on Online Platforms" by the European Law Institute (ELI) (September 2019),[34] Omnibus Directive,[35] "A European strategy for data" (February 2020),[36] etc., were published.

In the following, this chapter focuses on the Online Intermediation Services Regulation and the European strategy for data, addressing issues related to the transfer and distribution of data.

2.2 *Online Intermediation Services Regulation*

2.2.1 Outline

The Regulation on the Promotion of Fairness and Transparency of Online Intermediation Services for Business Users (hereinafter referred to as the "P2B Regulation"), entering into force on July 12, 2020, was enacted to ensure that business users of

---

[22] Regulation (EU) 2017/745.

[23] https://digital-strategy.ec.europa.eu/en/library/summary-report-public-consultation-evaluation-directive-969ec-legal-protection-databases.

[24] Regulation (EU) 2018/302.

[25] COM (2018) 1177.

[26] COM (2018) 236.

[27] For an overview of the Code, see *infra* note 45.

[28] COM (2017) 495.

[29] Directive (EU) 2018/1972.

[30] Directive (EU) 2019/770.

[31] Directive (EU) 2019/771. For a Japanese translation, see Antonios Karaiskos, Yo Terakawa & Keita Baba (trans.) "Directive (EU) 2019/771 of the European Parliament and of the Council on certain aspects of contracts for the sale of goods" Nomos 45 (2019), p. 161 et seq.

[32] Directive (EU) 2019/1024.

[33] Regulation (EU) 2019/1150.

[34] It would be instructive to compare the P2B Regulation with the ELI's model rules. The ELI's report is available at https://www.europeanlawinstitute.eu/fileadmin/user_upload/p_eli/Publications/ELI_Model_Rules_on_Online_Platforms.pdf.

[35] Directive (EU) 2019/2161.

[36] COM (2020) 66.

online intermediation services and online search engines are provided with appropriate transparency, fairness and effective legal remedies (Article 1).[37] Before the passage of the P2B Regulation, there was years of debate over its proposal in the EU,[38] along with the establishment of an expert group to monitor online platforms.[39] The P2B Regulaiton formed a major pillar of EU online platform regulations, although it is not directly aimed at data transfer and distribution, which is the main subject of this chapter.

2.2.2 Purpose

The purpose of the P2B Regulation is to ensure that business users of online intermediation services and business users with respect to online search engines are afforded appropriate transparency and fairness (fairness) and effective redressability (Article 1).

A foundamental difference could be found between the P2B Regulation and the GDPR. Article 20 of the GDPR lays down the principle of data transfer with the aim of promoting the development of new services in the context of the Digital Single Market Strategy. Specifically, it confers rights to data subjects and giving them more control over their own personal data, supporting the free circulation of personal data within the EU, and promoting competition among controllers[40] between multiple service providers. In comparison, the P2B Regulation establishes a principle of transparency, which is based on the premise of data transfer.

2.2.3 Scope of Application

The P2B Regulation applies to online intermediation services and online search engines that are currently offered or will be offered to the following persons, regardless of the place of establishment of the online intermediation service provider or

[37] For an overview and a Japanese translation of the P2B Regulation, see Antonios Karaiskos, Yo Terakawa & Keita Baba, "Regulation (EU) 2019/1150 of the European Parliament and of the Council on promoting fairness and transparency in online intermediation services for business users: overview and article translation," NBL No. 1163 (2020), p. 34 et seq.

[38] From September 2015 to January 2016, a public consultation on the regulatory environment for platforms, online intermediaries, data and cloud computing and the collaborative economy was conducted. The original draft of the P2B Regulation was published in May 2016 in a Communication (COM (2016) 288) from the Commission to the European Parliament, the Council, the European Economic and Social Committee and the Committee of the Regions.

[39] Decision on setting up a group of experts for the Observatory on the Online Platform Economy (April 2018). The experts consisted of 15 independent academic members.

[40] The promotion of competition through the development of data transfer and opening rules is emphasized. For example, the aforementioned Framework Regulation for the Free Flow of Non-Personal Data within the EU (COM (2017) 495) also states that the ability to transfer data without hindrance is an important factor in promoting user choice and effective competition in the data processing services market.

online search engine provider: first, business users and corporate website users having their place of establishment or domicile in the EU; second, business users and corporate website users who provide goods or services to consumers located in the EU through online intermediation services or online search engines. The scope of "online intermediation services" here is defined as services that meet all of the following requirements: (a) information society services within the meaning of Article 1(1)(b) of Directive (EU) 2015/1535, i.e., services provided by remote and electronic means for remuneration at the individual request of the recipient of the services; (b) services enabling business users to provide goods or services to consumers in order to facilitate the initiation of direct transactions between the business user and the consumer, regardless of whether the transactions are ultimately successful or not; (c) services that are provided to the business user on the basis of a contractual relationship in which the service provider is one party and the business user are the other party (Article 2(2)). The term "online search engine" means a digital service that searches, in principle, all or specific language websites on any subject based on a query, by keywords, phrases or other forms of input, and returns information related to the requested content (Article 2(5)).

With regards to the scope of business users, the P2B Regulation defines it as natural or legal persons who provide goods or services to consumers through online intermediation services for the purpose of trade, business, craft or profession (Article 2(1)). In addition, a "provider of online intermediation services" is a natural or legal person that currently provides or will provide online intermediation services to business users (Article 2(3)).

2.2.4 Main Content of the P2B Regulation

The content of the P2B Regulation focuses on the obligations of online intermediation services. First, Article 3 sets forth, among other things, the clarification of the terms and conditions to be ensured by online intermediation service providers. The terms and conditions must be drafted in plain and understandable language and be readily available to business users at all stages of the transaction. They must also include the grounds for any decision to suspend or restrict services, information on potentially related programs, and information regarding the effects of the terms and conditions on the business user's intellectual property rights. Article 4 provides for the restriction, suspension, and cessation of online intermediation services. Article 5 deals with the ranking determined by online intermediation services. Online intermediation service providers and online search engine providers are required to provide reasons for their ranking parameters in the terms and conditions of the contract. They are required to use plain and understandable terms and to keep their descriptions up-to-date. If any remuneration paid by business users or other parties influences the rankings, the possibility of this being the case must also be stated. If a third party's notification leads to a revision of the ranking order or a removal from the search results, the online search engine provider must provide the corporate website users with an opportuinty to confirm the contents of the notification.

The most noteworthy provision in the P2B Regulation is Article 9. Subject to Article 20 of the GDPR (data portability)[41] and Article 6 of the Regulation on a framework for the free flow of non-personal data in the European Union (porting of data),[42] Article 9(1) of the P2B Regulation states that online intermediation service providers must make clear in their terms and conditions the technical and contractual access or prohibition of access by business users to personal data or other data provided by business users or consumers, or generated through such services, or both. Paragraph 2 of the same Article imposes notification obligations on the online intermediation service providers. The first of the obligations is whether and under what conditions the online intermediation service provider may access data and the type of data to be accessed, i.e., whether the online intermediation service provider has access to personal or other data, or both, provided by business users or consumers for the use of its services or generated through the provision of those services, and if so, what type of data can be accessed and under what conditions. The second is whether and under what conditions business users may access data, and the types of data accessed, i.e., data provided by that the business user in connection with the use of the online intermediation service concerned, or that generated through the provision of those services to that business user and the consumers of the business user's goods or services. The third concerns access by business users to aggregated data, i.e., whether business users have access to personal data or other data, or both, in aggregate form, and if so, under what conditions and to what types of data. The fourth concerns the provision of data to third parties (data sharing), i.e., whether data will be provided to third parties, the purpose of such data sharing, and if the provision of such data to third parties is not necessary for the proper functioning of the online intermediation service, The business user must be informed of information specifying the purpose of such data sharing and the option to opt out of such data sharing.

(5) Comparison of the P2B Regulation and the Corresponding Japanese law.

In Japan, Act on Enhancing Transparency and Fairness of Specified Digital Platforms (TFDPA), a law corresponding to the P2B Regulation, was passed and came into force in 2020.[43] Under this Act, businesses providing digital platforms where a high need for enhancing the transparency and fairness of transactions is identified may be designated as "specified digital platform providers" based on a Cabinet Order, regardless of whether they are domestic or foreign. A specified digital platform provider is required to (i) notify information about its terms and conditions of transactions, (ii) autonomously establish procedures and systems based on principles prescribed by the Minister of Economy, Trade and Industry (METI), and (iii) report

---

[41] See *infra* note 49.

[42] With a view to encouraging and facilitating the development of codes of conduct as self-regulation at EU level, based on the principles of transparency and interoperability and taking into account open standards, in order to contribute to a competitive data economy, Article 6 encourages the switching of service providers and the porting of data in a structured, commonly used and machine-readable format including open standard formats where required or requested by the service provider receiving the data.

[43] Law No. 38 of June 3, 2020.

and evaluate the status of operation (annually submit a report, including the status of (i) and (ii) and a self-evaluation thereof, to the METI, who will evaluate the operation status based on the report and publish the evaluation results).

Concerning the differences between these two laws, under the TFDPA, the classification and scale of the business is designated by a Cabinet Order, while the P2B Regulation does not stipulate the scale of the business. Moreover, the TFDPA covers large-scale online malls and app stores. By contrast, the P2B Regulation covers search engine services, which is at present not covered in the TFDPA. However, it is possible under the TFDPA to further cover search engine services with a government ordinance.

2.3 *European Data Strategy 2020*[44]

The EU report titled "A European strategy for data" provides an overview about the EU's data strategy, which aims to promote the development and implementation of artificial intelligence and new businesses, to strengthen EU's international competitiveness, and to reduce its environmental burden by building institutions and spaces for sharing industrial and administrative data of European companies. The report cites the following four points as the background to the report: (1) the increasing volume of data generated around the world and the rapid pace of technological change, such as edge computing; (2) the growing importance of data for businesses and consumers in the digital economy, and its potential to contribute to various social changes and solutions to problems; (3) the fact that the EU has a source of competitiveness in the data economy for the comingdecades, yet the EU is falling behind the U.S. and China in innovation; and (4) the EU has already had a variety of leading initiatives, including the GDPR, that have facilitated the development of the data economy. In addition to this, the goal of the EU's digital strategy is to create a European data space connected to data from all over the world. There, non-personal data, including sensitive business data, and personal data, will be protected, and companies will have almost unlimited access to high-quality industrial data. To achieve this vision, the common European rules and enforcement mechanisms should ensure that (i) data is transferable across sectors in the EU; (ii) European rules and values, in particular personal data protection, consumer protection and competition law, are fully respected; and (iii) the rules on access to and use of data are fair, practical and clear, and clear and trustworthy data governance mechanisms are in place.

On the other hand, the report also identifies actual and possible challenges to the EU's data strategy as follows. (i) The problem of data availability, in that there is currently not enough data for innovative reuse, including the development of artificial intelligence. (ii) The problem of imbalance among companies, in that the provision of cloud services and data infrastructure is concentrated in certain companies, and there is also imbalance in access to and use of data. (iii) Data interoperability, in which

[44] See, *supra* note 36.

free exchange of data from different sources within a sector or combining data across sectors is hindered by different standards, etc. (iv) Data governance, which requires an organizational approach and structure to enable data-driven innovation based on the existing legal framework. (v) Data infrastructure independency, which requires reducing the technological dependencies in other countries' cloud infrastructures, which is the heart of the data economy. (vi) The absence of technical tools and standards that facilitate individuals' exercising their rights under the GDPR and ePrivacy legislation. (vii) The issue of data processing skills and literacy, where the lack of data professionals and data literacy is significant and could weigh on the future of the data economy. (viii) Cybersecurity issues, as much data is spread closer to the user 'at the edge' rather than stored in data centers, which in turn makes data protection vulnerable.

In response to these challenges, the report lays out an agenda and process chart for a European data strategy. First, it states that cross-sectoral governance for data access and use should be considered. To this end, it proposes a legal framework for the governance of common European data spaces in 2020. If necessary, a Dataa Act will be submitted to the European Parliament in 2021. This is due to the fact that tackling online disinformation is expensive and inefficient due to the wide variation in national rules. Although the European Commission have published the Code of Practice on Disinformation, the lack of common, legally binding rules in the EU is still deemed problematic.[45] The momentum towards enacting this Data Act also stems from the fact, according to the report, that the interoperability of services should be improved, as mentioned above, in order to make higher quality public sector data available for reuse, taking into account its potential for European SMEs.

The second part of the agenda is to strengthen the data infrastructure in Europe. This means investing in relevant and high-impact projects on the European data spaces, specifically data sharing architectures and governance mechanisms (from 2022), signing Memoranda of Understanding with Member States on cloud collaboration (Q3 2020), and integrating all cloud services. The followings are to be done: to

[45] The EU Code of Conduct on Disinformation is a set of guidelines for signatories (online platform operators such as Google, Facebook, and Twitter) to prevent the spread of disinformation, including so-called fake news. Signatories are required to: (i) include safeguards against the provision of disinformation; (ii) improve inspection of ad placement to reduce the revenue of purveyors of disinformation; (iii) improve transparency regarding political and issue-based advertising, and from the perspective of enabling users to understand why they have been targeted by advertisements; (iv) implement or improve appropriate policies against misrepresentation; (v) enhance efforts to close fake accounts or present their effectiveness and establish clear marking systems and bot rules to ensure that their behavior is not confused with human interaction; (vi) that signatories must make efforts to guarantee the integrity of their services with regard to the issue of accounts aimed at spreading false information; (vii) invest in technological means to prioritize authenticated, accurate, and authorized information, in accordance with Article 10 of the European Convention on Human Rights and the principles of freedom of speech; (viii) ensure transparency to allow users to understand why they are being targeted by political or issue-based advertising; (ix) prevent disinformation from being exposed by improving the discoverability of credible content; (x) ensure that users have access to tools that allow for a customized and interactive online experience; (xi) take reasonable steps to ensure that privacy complainants have access to fact-checking data. As the phrase "shall endeavor to do so" indicates, this is only a non-binding obligation.

develop a European cloud services marketplace (Q4 2022), and to create a rulebook on (self-)regulated clouds in the EU (Q2 2022).

The third part on the agenda is to strengthen individual rights with regard to the use of the data they generate, and to increase investment in big-data related skills and SMEs. This includes strengthening individuals' right to data portability under Article 20 of the GDPR, and giving them more control over who can access and use their machine-generated data. These issues can be further explored in the context of the Data Act mentioned above.

3 Discussion on Data Transfer and Distribution in Japan[46]

3.1 Review of the Current Situation

What is ongoing in Japan with regard to data transfer and distribution? A guidance titled "Options for Ideal Approaches to Data Transfer and Disclosure" (hereinafter referred to as "Options") introduces examples of methods to achieve data transfer and disclosure.[47]

It is becoming increasingly important to have a mechanism that allows users (consumers) to freely, smoothly, and easily reuse the data accumulated on online platforms. Online platforms tend to accelerate the concentration of data across borders because they are two-sided markets where users of each side of the market gather spontaneously on the platform (direct and indirect network effects). On the other hand, these users do not necessarily act rationally based on all objective facts when they provide data to the platform. Therefore, a question may arise that whether it is necessary to offer these users an opportunity to transfer the data they have provided. However, it is critical that the rule of data transfer and disclosure should neither discourage innovation nor impede new entry, and that the rule should be designed with a view to facilitating the transaction and distribution of data. Three viable choices are illustrated in the Options. ① Data access: Company B may also access the user data held by Company A based on the user's instructions on the premise that Company A opens its APIs to Company B. ② Data disclosure: the user can first download data held by Company A, and then upload (transfer) the data to Company B. ③ Data transfer: Following the user's instructions, Company A directly duplicates

[46] Section 3 is basically an excerpt from the paper written by Shuya Hayashi, "Aspects of International Rule-Making Concerning Digital Platforms: The So-Called 'One Country, Two Systems' Issue and Legal Disciplines Concerning Data Transfer and Distribution," Nextcom, No. 41 (2020), p. 8.

[47] Ministry of Economy, Trade and Industry, Fair Trade Commission, and Ministry of Internal Affairs and Communications, Options for Ideal Approaches to Data Transfer and Disclosure (May 21, 2019).

the user data it holds to Company B and/or deletes the data when the duplication is completed.[48]

Regarding the transfer and distribution of data, in the EU the GDPR provides for the right to so-called data portability in Article 20, which stipulates the right to receive personal data in a structured, commonly used and machine-readable format and the right to transfer personal data directly from one data controller to another. The right to transfer[49] is stipulated, attaching rights to data subjects and giving them more control over their own personal data. This is expected to facilitate the free flow of personal data within the EU and promote competition among data controllers.[50] Similar in Japan, Article 28 of the Act on the Protection of Personal Information guarantees the right to demand disclosure of personal information from business operators handling personal information. Sector-specific regulations may also be involved. For example, in the financial sector, the revised Payment Services Directive[51] requires banks in the EU to disclose APIs to bank account payment service providers (include PISPs and AISPs). In Japan, the revised Banking Act[52] also aims to have all banks adopt open APIs by June 2020.

On the other hand, big data-related service providers are making voluntary efforts to respond to this issue. The Data Transfer Project ("DTP"), a joint project by Facebook, Google, Microsoft, and Twitter, has been attracting attention.[53] The DTP was launched in 2018 with the goal of building an open source data portability platform between services to allow all individuals using the web to easily move data between online service providers whenever they wish. To faciliatate the direct data transfer between services, the DTP focuses on the following issues the first issue is bandwidth. When the bandwidth is limited, downloading and uploading data often takes much time and is costly and impractical. The second issue is incompatible formats. Companies have begun to provide data in structured, commonly used, machine-readable formats (for whatever reason), but in most cases these formats are incompatible, making it difficult for users to re-import exported data. The third issue is discoverability. When data is exported, it is often difficult to know where else to take the data. Therefore, the DTP aims to enable direct transfer of data by establishing a format for data exchange and providing each data-related service with a mechanism using this format for output and input. Specific cases proposed the DTP include the

48 Options, p. 8.

49 However, this is limited to cases that are technically feasible.

50 See Executive Summary of Guidelines on the right to data portability.

51 Directive 2007/64/EC, replaced by PSD2.

52 Act to Amend the Banking Act, etc. (Act No. 49 of 2017).

53 https://datatransferproject.dev.

transfer of photo data (SNS to print service),[54] the transfer of playlists between music services,[55] and the transfer of customer purchase and point data between stores.[56]

However, it should be noted that the UK Competition and Markets Authority has issued a report stating that the cases currently proposed by the DTP alone are unlikely to have a decisive effect on improving competition.[57]

3.2 Discussion Points[58]

The transfer and distribution of data involve various issues. Based on the "Options" mentioned above, the following issues may arise.

3.2.1 Scope of Target Businesses

If data transfer and disclosure rules are to be established, should the target businesses be broadly defined to include all businesses that provide digital platforms, or should certain threshold be set for them? If a certain threshold is to be set, then the issue moves to what kind of indicators would be appropriate to use, such as those with user data above a certain size, or those with sales above a certain size.

3.2.2 Scope of Services to Be Covered

Should services, such as social networking, online shopping, search services, app stores, and message delivery, be considered respectively? In doing so, should we take into account what kind of data is held by online platform operators in accordance with each different service? Also, should online intermediation services cover not only BtoBtoC services but also CtoBtoC services?

---

[54] When a user's photos are stored on their social media accounts, she can access the website or app provided by the photo printing service to initiate a direct transfer from the social media platform to the photo printing service.

[55] If a user does not agree with the privacy policy of a music service and wants to stop using it immediately, but does not want to lose the playlists she has created, she is allowed to use the original provider's export function to save a copy of his playlists to the cloud DTP is a simple and easy way to create a new playlist. This would allow the user to import the list to a new provider or multiple providers.

[56] If a supermarket trade association wants to allow customers (consumers) to transfer their loyalty card data from one store to another where currently they are members and get coupons based on their purchasing habits at each store, the association can host an industry-specific DTP platform.

[57] The UK Competition and Markets Authority published the interim report "Online platforms and digital advertising market study" on December 18, 2019. See Appendix L, "Personal data. Potential Approaches for Improving Mobility", which mentions the DTP in 6.135.

[58] See "Options," p. 5 et seq.

3.2.3 Scope of Target Users

Should individual users and business users be covered without distinction? In addition to those who receive services via the online platform, should the service provider (store owners, advertisers, etc.) be also subject to the same rule?

3.2.4 Details of Data Transfer and Disclosure Rules

This can be further divided into six categories: (1) types of data to be covered, (2) categories of the covered data, (3) methods of data transfer and distribution, (4) formats for data transfer and distribution, (5) development of the data reciver's systems, and (6) the issue of sharing the cost burden.

With respect to (1), what should be the scope of the types of data to be covered? Specifically, in addition to personal data, should data generated by users (e.g., digital content) be covered even if it does not fall into the scope of personal data? Should data provided by legal entities also be covered? With respect to (2), how should the scope be set with respect to the categories of the covered data? Specifically, should it include observed data, which are indirectly provided by users when they use services provided by online platform operators[59]? Furthermore, should it include data generated by online platform operators through the analysis of the data provided directly or indirectly by users? For (3), the aforementioned " data access", " data disclosure", and "data transfer" are available methods. Regarding (4), is it necessary to standardize the format? However, since standardization of data formats is fraught with difficulty when there are numerous parties involved, it may be a more practical and feasible way to promote services that enable compatibility of data specifications by means of disclosing data specifications in conjunction with data disclosure. With regard to (5), the question is how to ensure data security. If data is to be transferred to a third party, should such third party be required to have a system in place for information security? For example, is it required to transfer data to a place where the system for information security is confirmed to be in place for the handling of information, such as information bank[60]? Regarding (6), the issue is whether only business operators should bear the development and operation cost of a system that enables data transfer and disclosure. If data transfer and disclosure rules are established not from the perspective of individual rights but from the perspective of competition, it is an issue whether it is necessary to require those who request data transfer/disclosure to bear the costs. Furthermore, another issue is whether only business operators should bear the costs incurred in response to individual data

[59] The GDPR covers personal data relating to oneself that one has provided to a controller, specifically, not only data provided by oneself, but also observational data provided through the use of services or equipment (but not including data inferred or derived from the analysis of the data provided) (see Guidelines on the Right to Data Portability III).

[60] METI, Study Group on the Scheme for Accreditation of Information Trust Functions, "Guidelines for Accreditation of Information Trust Functions Ver 2.0" (2019).

transfer/disclosure requests, or whether it should be allowed to pass on some of the costs to those who request data transfer/disclosure.

3.2.5 Approaches to Achieve Data Transfer and Distribution

What specific approaches could be taken to achieve this, such as legislation, co-regulation, and self-regulation?

3.3 Considerations

As previously discussed, issues have been raised regarding the transfer and distribution of data. The authors would then like to focus on the necessity and purpose of data transfer and disclosure rules in the following section.

3.3.1 Necessity and Purpose of Data Transfer and Disclosure Rules

The necessities and purposes of data transfer and opening rules are diverse. However, In view of foreign legislations on this subject, there seems to be a consensus that such rules are a tool for competition policy and innovation (open innovation). Further, it is important to acknowledge that in the EU the protection of natural persons in relation to the processing of personal data is defined as a fundamental right, as mentioned above. In addition, the authors would like to emphasize the importance of the aspect of consumer protection. Apart from the limited rationality of consumers, there is asymmetry[61] between consumers and online platform operators in terms of both information on how data is collected and used by online platform operators and recognition of the value of data. Even if consumers were able to precisely recognize the use of data by online platform operators, it would be impossible for them to monitor how the operators are using the data. In view of this asymmetry, the author believes that the relationship between the depositor (who provide the data) and the receiver (who analyze the data) is consistent with the concept of information fiduciary,[62] i.e., "a framework of a trust-like relationship when users entrust their information to the counterparty."[63,64] The concept of "information fiduciary" would be further explained later (see (2)).

[61] Acquisti et al. (2016).

[62] For the definition and concept of information fiduciary, see, Richards (2015), Balkin (2016), Dobkin (2018). For references in Japanese, see, Saito (2018).

[63] Keigo Komamura, "Symposium 'Law as a Principle of Reconstruction, and Architecture (Part.1)'," Hōgaku Seminā, No. 690 (2012), p. 37.

[64] In this regard, Saito (2019), provides a detailed discussion of the relevant arguments.

In the world of competition law, there is a view that the so-called essential facility (EF) doctrine provides the theoretical grounds for the transfer and disclosure rules. However, Big Data in most cases lacks these two elements: (1) the indispensability of the EF, and (2) the finite scarcity of resources (depending on the type of data, though).[65] On the other hands, in the financial sector, for example, since PSPs (payment service providers) need to go through accounts at financial institutions when conducting foreign exchange transactions, accounts at financial institutions may constitute an EF in this sense. Given that unreasonable conditions may be imposed on the PSPs when they access accounts at financial institutions, the applicability of the EF doctrine should not be completely denied so as to maintain a level playing field. Also, the public interest should be taken into account on a case-by-case basis. In Japan, the Next Generation Medical Infrastructure Act[66] provides a special exception to the Personal Information Protection Law, allowing medical institutions to provide authorized business operators with medical information, which is personal information requiring special consideration, because of the public interest in medical data.

3.3.2 Applicability of the Theory of Information Fiduciary

Below is an introduction to the concept of "information fiduciary" and its theoretical ground from Jack M. Balkin,[67] the main proponent of this concept. Information fiduciary refers to a position held by persons or companies, mainly professionals such as doctors, lawyers, accountants and investment advisors, that assume special responsibility for information obtained based on a fiduciary relationship with the counterparty. The fiduciary relationship itself is not a new concept, but in the digital age, the relationship between the online platform operator and the end user should be defined as a new kind of fiduciary relationship. By doing so, the legal principles that have long recognized in the fiduciary relationship could be applied in the context of information fiduciary.

The following four elements can be considered to be the grounds of the fiduciary relationship. The first is the asymmetry of position and information between end users and online platform operators. While end users have practical difficulty in monitoring the behavior of online platform operators and prevent the operators from acting in ways that harm their interests or betray their trust, it is relatively easy for online platform operators to monitor the end users' behavior by collecting massive information from them via the platform. The second is the end users' dependence on online platform operators. When the online platform operator offers a service

[65] There are several papers that argue the EF theory may be appropriate if the personal data held by a company is essential to facilitate market access for other players in a specific industry, such as online social networks, online search, or online advertising (e.g., Vanberg and Uenver (2017)). These arguments however do not seem to be prevailing.

[66] Act on Anonymously Processed Medical Information to Contribute to Research and Development in the Medical Field., Act No. 28 of 2009.

[67] Balkin, *supra* note 62.

indispensable to its end-users, and the users have no alternative but to use the service, the users have no other option but to expect the platform operator's "decent behavior" so that they will not be disadvantaged by the operator's misuse or leakage of the users' information. The third is the special expertise of online platform operators. In other words, in exchange for the end-user's personal information, online platform operators are acting as professionals and should be thus treated in same manner. The fourth is the importance of trust in the online platform operator. Put differently, it is recognized that online platform operators should behave as trusted institutions that act consistently with the end users' interests, even if they pursue profit.

These four elements are the reasons why end-users, in their vulnerable position, demand that online platform operators offer safe and secure services. In response, platform operators should endeavor to act as trustworthy collectors and custodians of personal information, and attempt to build relationships with end-users based on trust given that they cannot guarantee complete transparency in their business for the sake of cyber security and business competitivenessip. In view of this relationship, Balkin states that a new kind of fiduciary relationship in the information society should be admitted. Ariel Dobkin further this concept and lists four principles as norms to be followed by businesses that fall under the category of information fiduciary.[68] The first is the anti-manipulation of the users, which means that the online platform operator's own interests should not be prioritized over the interests of the users.[69] The second is anti-discrimination. It prohibits discrimination among users on the grounds of race, gender, etc.[70] The third is limited sharing with third parties. In other words, it may be allowed for online platform operators to provide user information they collect from users to subsidiaries or affiliate companies in the same group, but not to advertisers, and aggregators (companies that collect, organize, and provide information to third parties) cannot be the subject of information fiduciary, and businesses subject to information fiduciary must neither provide personal information to aggregators nor recieve information from aggregators.[71] The fourth is that they must not violate their own privacy policies. This is because it is the reasonable expectation of users that a business will not violate the privacy policy it has created for itself. Such an expectation is concerned with the overall INFORMATION FIDUCIARY DUTY.

---

[68] Dobkin, *supra* note 62.

[69] For example, if Facebook. were to provide only certain groups of users (those who support the candidate that Zuckerberg supports) with a button declaring that they have already voted, including a link to locate their polling place, during an election, it would be making a distinction based on preference, and the principle of fair treatment is violated because it violates the reasonable expectation and trust of users that the algorithm will be applied equally to all users.

[70] This principle is violated, for example, when Facebook grants a newsfeed function and posting privileges only to people who earn above a certain income level or have a specific job in a certain field, or when Facebook acquires a mortgage lender and subsidiaries it, and then provides its credit officers with information about users' Facebook and social networks and allows them to use the information to evaluate whether to continue lending credit.

[71] For example, targeting a particular critic in the use of Uber, examining data collected from his or her service use history, and then reciprocating with a blog to discredit that critic when he or she writes an essay criticizing Uber, would violate this principle.

This concept of information fiduciary is being applied to legislation as well. For example, the New York State Privacy Bill has an information fiduciary provision.[72] In Article 1102 of the bill, it defines data fiduciary as: "Personal data of consumers shall not be used, processed or transferred to a third party, unless the consumer provides express and documented consent. every legal entity, or any affiliate of such entity, and every controller and data broker, which collects, sells or licenses personal information of consumers, shall exercise the duty of care, loyalty and confidentiality expected of a fiduciary with respect to securing the personal data of a consumeragainst a privacy risk; and shall act in the best interests of the consumer, without regard to the interests of the entity, controller or data broker, in a manner expected by a reasonable consumer under the circumstances."

On the other hand, in Japan, the court held in the Yahoo Japan Auction case that the defendant (Yahoo Japan) had an obligation to the users, including the plaintiffs, to build a defect-free system and provide the service on the basis of good faith and fair dealing.[73] The specific details of the obligation, according to the decision, are determined by comprehensively considering the social conditions surrounding Internet auctions at the time the service was provided, relevant laws and regulations, the technical level of the system, the cost of building and maintaining the system, the effects of the introduction of the system, and the convenience of the system users. The issue for the near future is how to develop and control the implications of this obligation derived from good faith and fair dealing. As to legislative measures, such as the aforementioned New York State Privacy Bill, they may be a possible solution but need a thorough review.

4 Conclusion

This chapter provides an introduction and some discussion of international discipline on online platform operators, focusing on the debate surrounding data transfer and distribution. This is an issue that needs to be considered internationally from a interdisciplinary, and cross-agency perspective. On the other hand, while this chapter has limited discussion on this issue from the perspective of competition law, research reports and policy recommendations in this area, e.g., EC Directorate-General for Competition, "Competition Policy in the Digital Age" (April 2019, the so-called

[72] The Bill (S5642) has been introduced in the Senate Consumer Protection Committee. The substantially same bill (A8526) has also been introduced in the House Committee on Consumer Affairs and Protection. https://www.nysenate.gov/legislation/bills/2019/s5642 and https://www.nysenate.gov/legislation/bills/2019/a8526 (viewed May 1, 2020).

[73] Nagoya District Court, March 28, 2008, Hanrei Jiho No. 2029, p. 89.

"Crémer" report)[74] and German Federal Ministry of Economics, "New Competition Framework for the Digital Economy" (September 2019),[75] have been published in rapid succession by national competition authorities globally. Thus, it is also important to strengthen the oversight (monitoring) of the data-related industry by competition authorities.[76] The University of Chicago Stigler Commission Report (September 2019) calls for strengthening the regulatory authority of the U.S. FTC (Federal Trade Commission) to curb market dominance by data. The report also envisions the creation of a "Digital Authority" as a long-term agenda. The silimar "Digital Authority" concept is also proposed by the UK House of Lords in March 2019. These recommendations are worthy of consideration.

5 Summary

This chapter provides an introduction and overview of the international rules for online platform operators, focusing on recent developments in the EU and the debate surrounding data transfer and distribution. The EU's social and economic digitization policy can be divided into three periods. As for the Online Intermediation Services Regulation, it does not directly cover data transfer and distribution, but it is a major pillar of the EU's online platform regulation; the content of the P2B Regulation focuses on the obligations of online intermediation services; and the EU Data Strategy is a report titled "European Strategy for Data," which outlines how the EU aims to develop and realize artificial intelligence and new businesses, strengthen the EU's international competitiveness, and reduce its environmental footprint by building institutions and fora for sharing industrial and administrative data of European companies. It is vital that the discussion on data transfer and distribution in Japan be designed from the perspective of facilitating trade and distribution of data, with respect to data transfer and distribution. On the other hand, big data-related service providers are making voluntary efforts to address this issue. Discussion points regarding data transfer and distribution include (1) the scope of target service providers, (2) the scope of target services, (3) the scope of target users, (4) the content of data transfer and disclosure rules, and (5) the approach to realize transfer and distribution. This chapter focuses on the need for and purpose of data transfer and disclosure rules. The relationship between the depositor who provides data and the receiver who analyzes the data is considered consistent with the concept of information fiduciary, or "the framework of a trust relationship in which a user

[74] Competition Policy for the digital era, at https://ec.europa.eu/competition/publications/reports/kd0419345enn.pdf (viewed May 1, 2020).

[75] Ein neuer Wettbewerbsrahmen für die Digitalwirtschaft Bericht der Kommission Wettbewerbsrecht 4.0 (2019), at https://www.bmwi.de/Redaktion/DE/Publikationen/Wirtschaft/bericht-der-kommission-wettbewerbsrecht-4-0.pdf?__blob=publicationFile&v=12 (viewed May 1, 2020).

[76] Stigler Committee on Digital Platforms Final Report (2019), at https://research.chicagobooth.edu/-/media/research/stigler/pdfs/digital-platforms---committee-report---stigler-center.pdf?la=en&hash=2D23583FF8BCC560B7FEF7A81E1F95C1DDC5225E (viewed May 1, 2020).

entrusts his or her information to a partner." Also, with respect to the applicability of the information fiduciary theory, the position and information asymmetry between end users and online platform operators, end users' dependence on online platform operators, the expertise of online platform operators, and the importance of trust in the online platform operator, are mentioned. This concept of information fiduciary is increasingly being applied to laws, such as the New York State privacy bill.

References

Acquisti A, Taylor C, Wagman L (2016) The economics of privacy. J Econ Lit 54:442–492

Balkin JM (2016) Information fiduciaries and the first amendment. UC Davis Law Rev 49(4):1183–1234

Dobkin A (2018) Information fiduciaries in practice: data privacy and user expectations. Berkeley Technol Law J 33(1)

Hayashi S (2017) Zero-rating and network neutrality. J Inf Commun Policy 1(1):19

Richards N (2015) Intellectual privacy. Oxford University Press

Saito K (2018) Privacy protection as a duty of confidence. J Inf Commun 36(2):127

Saito K (2019) 'Autonomy' and 'trust' in privacy. J Inf Commun Policy 3(1): II–1

Vanberg A, Uenver MB (2017) The right to data portability in the GDPR and EU competition law: odd couple or dynamic duo? Eur J Law Technol 8(1):1–22

Chapter 7
Digital Platform Regulation

1 Purpose of this Chapter

This chapter addresses various aspects of international rule-making concerning digital platforms. First, the so-called "one country, two systems" issue regarding the application and enforcement of laws in Internet services will be discussed, using the Telecommunications Business Law (hereinafter in this chapter referred to as 'TBL') and the Act on the Protection of Personal Information (hereinafter in this chapter referred to as 'APPI') as examples. Second, legal rules on data transfer and distribution will be discussed, focusing on a recent government guidance titled "Options for Ideal Approaches to Data Transfer and Disclosure".[1]

2 The So-Called "One Country, Two Systems" Issue Under the TBL

2.1 What is the "One Country, Two Systems" Issue?

In the case that a certain service is provided to Japanese consumers, ① when the law applicable to the service that is provided from Japan is different from that provided from abroad, or ② Japanese laws are not applied in an enforceable manner, the so-called "one country, two systems" issue arises. In particular, since Internet services are often provided across national borders, the "one country, two systems" issue is likely to occur nowadays. In these circumstances, it has been pointed out that Japanese consumers and companies may be greatly disadvantaged due to different consumer protection rules, different competition conditions, or other reasons. A well-known

[1] Ministry of Economy, Trade and Industry, Fair Trade Commission, and Ministry of Internal Affairs and Communications, Options for Ideal Approaches to Data Transfer and Disclosure (May 21, 2019).

S. Hayashi and K. Arai, *Digitalization and Competition Policy in Japan*,
https://doi.org/10.1007/978-981-99-5310-3_7

example is that, under the former Consumption Tax Law, there were differences in taxation of services provided via the Internet, depending on the place of service. This is because the criterion for determining whether the provision of services, such as distribution of e-books, music, and advertisements via telecommunication lines (Internet, etc.), constitutes a domestic transaction subject to consumption tax (the so-called "inside/outside criterion") used to be the location of the business office where the person providing the services was located or registered. However, the Act for Partial Revision of the Income Tax Act, etc. (Act No. 9 of 2015) amended the Consumption Tax Act, and the criterion for determining whether a service is internal or external was revised from the registered location of the business office to "the address, etc. of the person receiving the services." In this example, the "one country, two systems" issue existed in the sense that there was no equal footing in terms of law application, and this issue was eventually solved by legislation.[2]

2.2 An Issue of Equal Footing Concerning the Law Enforcement of the TBL

On the other hand, another typical example of the "one country, two systems" issue exists in the the current TBL. In terms of law application, the TBL is theoretically applicable equally to foreign carriers ("a carrier that provides telecommunications services in Japan without having telecommunications facilities in Japan") as well as domestic carriers. However, in terms of law enforcement, there is a problem that Japanese law is not enforceable against foreign carriers in practice. This problem is pointed out in the Final Report on Comprehensive Review of Competition Rules in the Telecommunications Business Sector (hereinafter "Comprehensive Verification Final Report"),[3] which was published by the Information and Communications Council, a special committee of the Ministry of Internal Affairs and Communications (MIC). According to the report, "the current TBL in Japan does not apply to carriers (including foreign platform operators) that install facilities outside Japan and provide services for the domestic market. In other words, the rules of the TBL (market entry rules, secrecy of communications, reporting of business suspension, etc.), which apply to domestic carriers providing telecommunications services, do not apply to those who provide equivalent services from outside Japan to domestic users. This has brought about inequity in the application of the law between domestic

[2] National Tax Agency, Review of Taxation of Consumption Tax on Cross-border Provision of Services, etc. (May 2015).

[3] Information and Communications Council, Final Report of the Comprehensive Review of Competition Rules in the Telecommunications Business Sector (Consultation No. 25, December 17, 2018).

and foreign operators in Japan's telecommunications market, and provided inadequate protection for domestic users." "It is necessary to examine the legal rules and measures applied to foreign carriers in the Japanese telecommunications sector."[4]

With respect to jurisdiction, there are generally two kinds of issues to be considered. One is the issue of prescriptive jurisdiction, which is discussed from the perspective of whether the laws of one's own country can be applied to violations of such laws committed outside one's own territory. The other is the issue of executive jurisdiction, which is discussed from the perspective of whether the authority can be exercised over businesses located in a foreign country.[5] However, it seems unclear which issue is the target of the report, if only judging from the previous quote. In this regard, the report[6] states, "in applying the TBL to foreign carriers, in addition to the perspective of equal footing with domestic carriers, there are also issues in applying administrative measures and penalties, which are the exercise of public authority, to foreign carriers due to the constraint on executive jurisdiction. To address these issues in light of the assurance of effective enforcement is thus necessary." It is accordingly clear that the discussion in the report is focused on executive jurisdiction.

Although the TBL is generally based on the principle of territoriality, it may be, in theory, applicable under the objective aspect of territorial jurisdiction as long as any party who receives the provision of services is located (based) in Japan, even if the facilities are located outside Japan. However, Japanese government has expressed its official views on this issue, confirming that the prscriptive jurisdiction under the TBL depends on whether the location where the facilities are installed, controlled or managed is in Japan. Specifically, (1) the focus of the TBL is mainly on the telecommunications facilities, but there is no specific limitation on the location of telecommunications facilities in the TBL. (2) Even if a person installs telecommunications facilities (servers, etc.) outside Japan, the TBL may apply to the person in the case that the person intermediates other persons' communications through the use of the telecommunications facilities insomuch as the person has a domestic base and controls or manages such telecommunications facilities in Japan.[7] In contrast, (3) when the server is located outside Japan and the person does not control or manage the server in Japan, the TBL would not apply even if the person is engaged in business for the domestic market. For example, "Google has set up servers and other facilities outside Japan, and has been providing services directly to the domestic market. But given that Google Japan does not control or manage telecommunications facilities set up outside Japan, it is considered that the TBL does not apply."[8] Thus, it would be

---

[4] Id, pp. 33–34.

[5] Prescriptive jurisdiction is sometimes referred to as disciplinary jurisdiction or subject matter jurisdiction. As for executive jurisdiction, it is sometimes referred to as procedural jurisdiction because of its focus on the extent to which the procedural rules, such as service of process, are enforceable.

[6] *Supra note* 79, p. 38.

[7] See House of Councillors, Committee on General Affairs, Hiroomi Kira, Government Witness Statement. Proceedings of the 186th Diet Session, House of Councillors, Committee on General Affairs, No. 18 (May 13, 2014).

[8] Id.

wrong to interpret that the secrecy of communications, as stipulated in Article 4 of the TBL, is inapplicable in virtue of the principle of territoriality. Instead, it should be applied indiscriminately to both domestic and foreign carriers (Needless to say, provisions in the TBL that need to be examined from this perspective are not limited to "secrecy of communications"[9]). In other words, the prescriptive jurisdiction in Article 4 of the TBL extends to foreign carriers as long as they are based in Japan, even if their servers, etc. are located outside Japan. However, even if the prescriptive jurisdiction in Article 4 of the TBL extends to foreign carriers, it is difficult, from the viewpoint of executive jurisdiction, to apply the TBL to cases where the carrier has no base in Japan. If any administrative action is taken against the foreign carrier based outside Japan, it would conflict with the basic principle of executive jurisdiction, which means that no act constituting an exercise of public authority shall be performed in the territory of another country without the consent of the government of that country.[10] For example, when the MIC applies the TBL to a company located in a foreign country, it would be in conflict with the basic principle of international law to issue a business improvement order or other administrative measures (compulsory measures) to the company in the foreign country without obtaining the consent of that foreign country. In addition, MIC's administrative guidance, as part of the procedure for such compulsory measures, might also fall under the definition of "exercise of public authority without the consent of the government of the foreign country", and may be problematic under international law.[11]

Regarding this issue, the Nordion case,[12] though an antitrust violation case, can be considered as an example. of. In this case, Nordion, a Canadian manufacturer and distributor of the radioisotope Molybdenum-99 (Mo-99), which accounted for over half of the global production of Mo-99 as well as the majority of its sales, was charged with private monopolization for forcing two major Japanese customers to conclude a long-term requirements contract with Nordion. In this case, the addressee (Nodion) of the Recommendation Decision (administrative order) did not have a base in Japan, but the decision became effective since the copy of the decision was received by a Japanese attorney authorized by the respondent Nordion. The violation (the act of concluding a long-term requirements agreement) was committed in Japan. From the perspective of prescriptive jurisdiction, the Japanese Antimonopoly Act

[9] "Not only 'secrets of communications', but also the application of provisions concerning 'fairness of use,' 'notification of suspension and discontinuation of telecommunications services,' and 'reporting of suspension of services, etc.' are considered important." *Supra note* 79, p. 39.

[10] In the famous Lotus Case (1927), the then Permanent Court of International Justice held that "... the first and foremost restriction imposed by international law upon a State is that-failing the existence of a permissive rule to the contrary-it may not exercise its power in any form in the territory of another State. In this sense jurisdiction is certainly territorial; it cannot be exercised by a State outside its territory except by virtue of a permissive rule derived from international custom or from a convention." S.S. "Lotus," Judgment of September 7th, 1927, P. C. I. J. Ser. A. No. 10, p. 19.

[11] In the context of competition law, see, the Ministry of Economy, Trade and Industry's "Study Group on International Enforcement of Competition Laws, Interim Report" (June 25, 2008), p. 23 et seq.

[12] JFTC Recommendation Hearing Decision September 3, 1998, 1998 (Recommendation) No. 16 [Nodion], Vol. 45, p. 148.

(hereinafter in this chapter referred to as 'AMA') could be applied to the case, even if the principle of territoriality was adopted. In this sense, the case did not raise an issue of extraterritoriality. On the other hand, from the viewpoint of executive jurisdiction, the decision became effective only because the attorney authorized by the respondent happened to receive it, but not every case ends with a happy ending. In view of this, the 2002 Amendment to the AMA introduced provisions for service of documents on foreign business operators and for service by publication. Explicitly speaking, when a foreign violating business operator does not have a business base in Japan, as is the case with Nordion, it is still possible, at the (potential) addressee's discretion, to appoint an agent in Japan and authorize her to receive documents and other materials related to examination procedures under the AMA. The JFTC could then serve documents to such agent. However, in cases where the foreign violating business operator has not appointed an agent, service via the competent government agency of the foreign country or via the Japanese ambassador, minister, or consul stationed in that country under Article 70–17 of the AMA as applied *mutatis mutandis* pursuant to Article 108 of the Code of Civil Procedure (service in a foreign country), or service by publication pursuant to Article 70–18 of the AMA, shall be made.

In contrast, in the case of the current TBL, there are no such service provisions, including service by publication. In this regard, the Comprehensive Verification Final Report states in page 157 that, "measures to ensure enforcement of the law against platform operators outside Japan may include, for example, international enforcement cooperation and the appointment of a domestic agent, as seen in the EU's General Data Protection Regulation." It has already been reported in the press that the MIC, in response to the report, intends to amend the TBL to require companies to appoint a representative or agent in Japan so that they can serve business improvement orders, etc.[13] Such an amendment of the TBL is definitely needed. However, it seems to be insufficient to only amend the TBL. Even if it were possible to issue a business improvement order to a foreign operator by serving a copy of the order to the agent under the amendment of the TBL, the rules would not be sufficiently effective without corresponding measures when the order is not obeyed.[14] In this regard, in the case of the AMA, if the agent refuses to receive the order, there are corresponding provisions in the AMA, including service in a foreign country and service by publication, as mentioned above.[15]

[13] NHK News Web, "'Applying the TBL to Foreign Giant IT Companies' draft report to amend the law," https://www3.nhk.or.jp/news/html/20191206/.k10012205141000.html (accessed December 20, 2019). See also, Asahi Shimbun, December 21, 2019 (morning) ("Improvement order to overseas IT possible").

[14] "It is necessary to further examine whether simply requiring the addressee to appoint an authorized agent in Japan is sufficient or not." *Supra note* 79, p. 38.

[15] In a business combination case, the Japan Fair Trade Commission (JFTC) has served a report order by publication on a foreign operator that refused to accept a report order by service via the Japanese consul regarding the planned acquisition of a competing business, Rio Tinto, by an Australian resource company, BHP Billiton. See JFTC Secretary General's Press Conference, September 24, 2008.

Furthermore, it might be theoretically possible to impose indirect penalties for violation of an order, but, in the case of criminal penalties, interference with foreign sovereignty may be more serious than that in the case of administrative penalties. Besides, in the circumstances of refusal to receive the copy of the order, indirect penalties are not expected to be an effective against teh addressee, as a practical matter. In this regard, the MIC's "Final Report of the Study Group on Platform Services" (December 2019) states in page 9 that a sanctionary publication for acts in violation of the law will be introduced as an alternative sanction to criminal penalties. This could be regarded as a useful means to guarantee the effectiveness of law enforcement.

Nevertheless, there are countless real-world examples of huge amounts of data pertaining to the secrecy of communications of domestic users (Japanese citizens) being stored on foreign servers. The possibility cannot be denied that such data may be illegally leaked or stolen in foreign countries in the future. In such a case, since the illegal activity is completed outside Japan, if the operator is not based in Japan and does not manage or control telecommunication facilities in Japan, it may be impossible to exercise prescriptive jurisdiction from the perspective of the principle of territoriality (or objective territoriality), let alone executive jurisdiction in terms of the obligation to appoint an agent. On the other hand, if there is a leakage of a large amount of data of domestic users, the impact on the Japanese citizens could be enormous. In this case, it would be necessary to consider whether or not to modify the traditional territorial principle and adopt the so-called effect doctrine, which would apply the Japanese TBL even to an act completed in another country if it has a substantial impact on Japanese citizens or market. In any case, the discussion above is the legal issue concerning the cross-border application of the current TBL, and a legislative solution in a prompt manner is desirable.

3 A Justifiable Case of "One Country, Two Systems"—Cross-Border Data Transfer and Distribution Under the APPI

With respect to the "one country, two systems" issue, there are yet cases in which problems would arise if the applicable rules are not distinguished between those applied on domestic entities and those on foreign ones. For example, Article 24 of the APPI was introduced in 2015 to establish more prudent rules for the provision of personal information outside Japan by domestic businesses, aiming to protect the personal information and privacy of Japanese citizens. Article 23 of the APPI prior to the 2015 Amendment, which imposed restrictions on provision of personal data to third parties, laid down rules regarding the provision of personal data to third parties, but did not explicitly specify whether the third party herein was located in Japan or a foreign country. However, with the globalization of economic and social activities and the development of information and communication technology, the cross-border distribution of data containing personal information has been increasing rapidly, and the urgent need to establish rules for the transfer of personal data to foreign countries, as well as the need to ensure consistency with the international regulatory framework for the protection of personal information, has been stressed. For these reasons, a new provision on the provision of personal data to third parties in foreign countries was established in Article 24 of the APPI.[16]

Specifically, cross-border data distribution under Article 24 of the APPI is allowed if any one of the following conditions are met: (1) the third party concerned is located in a country specified by the Personal Information Protection Commission (PPC) according to Act on the Protection of Personal Information Enforcement Regulations (hereinafter referred to as "Regulations") as a country having a personal information protection system recognized to be of the same protection level as that of Japan, (2) where the third party concerned has established a system that meets the standards set forth in the Regulations as a system required for business operators handling personal information to establish when they continuously take necessary measures,[17] (3) where the third party falls under any of the items of Article 23(1) of the APPI, or (4) where the individual concerned has given her consent. (4) the person's consent.

It should be noted that Article 24 of the APPI should not be understood as a restriction on cross-border data distribution by requiring the consent of the individual for the provision of personal data resulting from "succession of business due to merger or other reasons."[18] Rather, Article 24 of the APPI should be rather understood as a response to the risk in the event of a cross-border M&A of a Japanese company by a foreign company that the foreign company might transfer Japanese personal information to abroad without any restrictions absent different domestic (Article 23) and foreign (Article 24) measures.

4 Regulations Concerning Data Transfer and Distribution

4.1 Review of the Current Situation

Apart from the issue of legal protection for domestic users in the case of cross-border distribution of data, as seen in the previous section, it is also becoming increasingly important to have a mechanism that allows users (consumers) to freely, smoothly,

---

[16] For an explanation of Article 24 of the APPI, see Personal Information Protection Commission, "Guidelines Concerning the APPI (PART of Foreign Third Party Provision)" (November 2016).

[17] Article 11–2 of the Regulations provides for a system that complies with the standards (standards for a system necessary to continuously take measures equivalent to those required to be taken by business operators handling personal information).

[18] Article 23(5) of the APPI: In the following cases, the person to whom the personal data concerned is provided shall not fall under the category of a third party with respect to the application of the provisions of the preceding paragraphs (omitted) (ii) Cases in which personal data is provided as a result of the succession of business due to merger or other reasons.

and easily reuse the data accumulated on digital platforms. Digital platforms tend to accelerate the concentration of data across borders they are two-sided markets where users of each side of the market gather spontaneously on the platform (direct and indirect network effects). On the other hand, these users do not necessarily act rationally based on all objective facts when they provide data to the platform. Therefore, a question may arise that whether it is necessary to offer these users an opportunity to transfer the data they have provided. However, it is critical that the rule of data transfer and disclosure should neither discourage innovation nor impede new entry, and that the rule should be designed with a view to facilitating the transaction and distribution of data. Three viable choices are illustrated in the "Options for Ideal Approaches to Data Transfer and Disclosure"[19] ① Data access: Company B may also access the user data held by Company A based on the user's instructions on the premise that Company A opens its APIs to Company B. ② Data disclosure: the user can first download data held by Company A, and then upload (transfer) the data to Company B. ③ Data transfer: Following the user's instructions, Company A directly duplicates the user data it holds to Company B and/or deletes the data when the duplication is completed.

Regarding the transfer and distribution of such data, for example, the EU General Data Protection Regulation (GDPR)[20] provides for the so-called right to data portability (Article 20), which stipulates the right to receive personal data in a structured, commonly used publicly available and machine-readable format and the right to transfer personal data directly from one data controller to another.[21] Article 20 attaches rights to data subjects and gives them more control over their own personal data. This is expected to facilitate the free flow of personal data within the EU and promote competition among data controllers.[22] Similar in Japan, Article 28 of the APPI guarantees the right to demand disclosure of personal information from business operators handling personal information. Sector-specific regulations may also be involved. For example, in the financial sector, the revised Payment Services Directive requires banks in the EU to disclose APIs to bank account payment service providers (include PISPs and AISPs). In Japan, the revised Banking Act also aims to have all banks adopt open APIs by June 2020. On the other hand, as a voluntary joint project, Facebook, Google, Microsoft and Twitter have launched Data Transfer Project (DTP) in 2018, aiming to enable direct data transfer by establishing a data exchange format for data portability and by providing each data-related service with a mechanism for data output and input with this format.

---

[19] *Supra note* 77.

[20] Regulation (EU) 2016/679 (OJ L 119, 4.5.2016, p. 1–88).

[21] However, this is limited to cases where it is technically feasible.

[22] See Guidelines on the right to data portability, Executive Summary.

4.2 *Discussion Points*[23]

The transfer and distribution of data is a broad topic with multiple perspectives that need to be considered. Namely, (1) the scope of covered entities (all or part of digital platforms), (2) the scope of covered services (SNS, online shopping, app stores, search services, etc.), (3) the scope of covered users, (4) the content of data transfer and disclosure rules, which can be further divided into six categories: (i) types of data to be covered (personal data, digital content, company data, etc.), (ii) categories of data to be covered (observed data, estimated/derived data, customer data, etc.), (iii) methods of data transfer and distribution (disclosure to users, direct transfer to other businesses, etc.), (iv) formats for data transfer and distribution (need for standardization, disclosure of data specifications, etc.), (v) development of the data receiver's systems, (vi) the issue of sharing the cost burden (the development and operation costs, costs incurred during individual transfer, etc.), and (5) approaches to achieve data transfer and distribution (laws and regulations, co-regulations, self-regulations, etc.). Approaches to achieve data transfer and distribution. Due to space limitations, this chapter focuses on the necessity and purpose of data transfer/distribution rules, and possible regulatory approaches.

4.3 *Necessity and Purpose of Data Transfer and Release Rules*

The necessities and purposes of data transfer and opening rules are diverse. However, in view of foreign legislations on this subject, there seems to be a consensus that such rules are a tool for competition policy and innovation (open innovation). Further, it is important to acknowledge that in the EU the protection of natural persons in relation to the processing of personal data is defined as a fundamental right, as mentioned above. In addition, the authors would like to emphasize the importance of the aspect of consumer protection. Apart from the limited rationality of consumers, there is asymmetry[24] between consumers and online platform operators in terms of both information on how data is collected and used by online platform operators and recognition of the value of data. Even if consumers were able to precisely recognize the use of data by online platform operators, it would be impossible for them to monitor how the operators are using the data. In view of this asymmetry, the authors believe that the relationship between the depositor (who provide the data) and the receiver (who analyze the data) is consistent with the concept of information fiduciary,[25] i.e., "a framework of a trust-like relationship when users entrust their

[23] *Supra note* 77, p. 5 et seq.

[24] Acquisti et al. (2016).

[25] For the definition and concept of information fiduciary, see, Richards (2015), Balkin (2016). (Professor Balkin argues that a duty of fiduciary duty (duty of care and duty of loyalty) should be

information to the counterparty."[26,27] It should not be ignored that there is also a strong skepticism about the fiduciary duty theory.[28] Certainly, the content of fiduciary duties is not clear, and the types of duties vary.[29] However, even if privacy is understood as "the right to control one's own information," an individual indeed has substantial difficulty in controlling their own information, which may be widely distributed online without her consent. The information fiduciary theory is even more convincing considering that individual end-users may become weary of controlling their own information and data. Additionally, in the Yahoo Japan Auction case,[30] it was held that the defendant (Yahoo Japan) had an obligation to the users, including the plaintiffs, to build a defect-free system and provide the service on the basis of good faith and fair dealing. The specific details of the obligation, according to the decision, are determined by comprehensively considering the social conditions surrounding Internet auctions at the time the service was provided, relevant laws and regulations, the technical level of the system, the cost of building and maintaining the system, the effects of the introduction of the system, and the convenience of the system users. The issue for the near future is how to develop and control the implications of this obligation derived from good faith and fair dealing.

In the world of competition law, there is a view that the so-called essential facility (EF) theory provides a theoretical ground for the data transfer and disclosure rules. However, Big Data in most cases lacks these two elements: (1) the indispensability of the EF, and (2) the finite scarcity of resources (depending on the type of data, though).[31] On the other hands, in the financial sector, for example, since PSPs (payment service providers) need to go through accounts at financial institutions when conducting foreign exchange transactions, accounts at financial institutions may constitute an EF in this sense. Given that unreasonable conditions may be imposed on the PSPs when they access accounts at financial institutions, the applicability of the EF theory should not be completely denied so as to maintain a level playing field. Also, the public interest should be taken into account on a case-by-case basis. In Japan, the Next Generation Medical Infrastructure Act[32] provides a special

imposed on digital platform operators like GAFA). Dobkin (2018) For references in Japanese, see Saito (2018).

[26] Keigo Komamura, "Symposium 'Law as a Principle of Reconstruction, and Architecture (Part.1),'" Legal Seminar No. 690, p. 37 (2012).

[27] In this regard, Saito (2019) provides an in-depth examination of the relevant arguments. Kunifumi Saito, "'Autonomy' and 'Trust' in Privacy," Information and Communication Policy Research, Vol. 3, No. 1, pp. II–1 (2019).

[28] Khan and Pozen (2019).

[29] See Higuchi (2019).

[30] Nagoya District Court, March 28, 2008, Hanrei Jiho No. 2029, p. 89.

[31] There are several papers that argue the EF theory may be appropriate if the personal data held by a company is essential to facilitate market access for other players in a specific industry, such as online social networks, online search, or online advertising (e.g., Vanberg and Uenver (2017)). These arguments however do not seem to be prevailing.

[32] Act on Anonymously Processed Medical Information to Contribute to Research and Development in the Medical Field, Act No. 28 of 2009.

exception to the Personal Information Protection Law, allowing medical institutions to provide authorized business operators with medical information, which is personal information requiring special consideration, because of the public interest in medical data.

4.4 *Regulatory Framework to Achieve Data Transfer and Distribution*

With respect to data transfer and distribution rules, what approach could be taken as a means to achieve this, such as legislation, co-regulation, or self-regulation? A "rule-based" approach, such as antitrust law and GDPR, and a so-called "principle-based" approach, which promote digital platform operators' voluntary efforts in the form that key principles and norms are set forth and expected to be followed explicitly by the digital platform operators. There are diverging opinions as to what kind of approach is desirable, but in addition to these two approaches, there is another approach—joint regulatory approach—that incorporates the characteristics of the two approaches. That is, instead of setting out specific rules in legislation, legislators clarify the basic principles, the grounds for regulation, and the subject matter of regulation in regulations, and business operators are encouraged to voluntarily draw up specific rules and guidelines enforce them jointly.

Concerning the joint regulatory approach, first, its feasibility should be further discussed and examined. Second, it is important that a wide range of stakeholders, including various digital platform operators and consumers (organizations), participate in formulating the joint regulation. It is far from enough for the government to merely assess self-regulations created by business associations. Commitment from consumers and users is particularly essential for the formulation of the joint regulation, especially given that self-determination by consumers in the form of "notice and choice," such as notification of terms and conditions of service provision and whether to agree to them or stop using the service, is becoming a mere formality.

5 Summary

This chapter addresses various aspects of international rulemaking regarding digital platforms. It examines the issue of the so-called "one country, two systems" regarding the application and enforcement of laws in Internet services, using TBL and APPI as examples. When a service is provided to Japanese consumers, the so-called "one country, two systems" issue arises when (1) the laws applicable to services provided from Japan differ from those applicable to services provided from overseas, and (2) Japanese law is not applied in an enforceable manner. From the perspective of law enforcement, there is the problem that Japanese law cannot be enforced in practice against foreign operators, and although the TBL is generally based on the principle of territoriality, the Japanese government has taken an official position on this issue and confirmed that jurisdiction under the TBL depends on whether the location where the facility is established, managed, and operated is in Japan. If a large amount of data of domestic users is leaked, the impact on Japanese citizens could be enormous. In this case, it would be necessary to consider whether to modify the traditional principle of territoriality and adopt the so-called effect principle, in which the Japanese TBL would apply even if an act is completed in another country provided that it has a substantial impact on Japanese nationals or markets. With regard to the one-country, two-country system issue, problems may also arise in some cases when the applicable rules do not distinguish between those for domestic and foreign entities. In addition to this, rules should also be considered with respect to regulations on data transfer and distribution. It is essential that the rules for data transfer and disclosure be designed from the perspective of facilitating data transactions and distribution, not from the perspective of hindering innovation or preventing new entrants.

References

Acquisti A, Taylor C, Wagman L (2016) The economics of privacy. J Econ Lit 54:442–492
Balkin JM (2016) Information fiduciaries and the first amendment. UC Davis L Rev 49:1185
Dobkin A (2018) Information fiduciaries in practice: data privacy and user expectations. Berkeley Tech L J 33:1
Higuchi N (2019) AI, robots, medicine, and the law. Musashino Law Rev 11(247)
Khan L, Pozen DE (2019) A skeptical view of information fiduciaries. Harv L Rev 133:497
Richards N (2015) Intellectual privacy. Oxford University Press
Saito K (2018) Trustworthiness. Privacy protection as an obligation. J Inf Commun 36(2):127
Vanberg A, Uenver MB (2017) The right to data portability in the GDPR and EU competition law: odd couple or dynamic duo? Eur J Law Technol 8(1):1–22

Chapter 8
Competition in Multisided Markets

1 Introduction

This chapter analyzes the multiple segments of private railways from a multisided-market perspective, which has often been earlier analyzed only from the perspective of business diversification.

The social background and impetus for the conception of this chapter are as follows. Recent developments in information and communication technology (ICT) have brought significant changes to both large and traditional industries. Three main issues are involved. First, what it means to dominate a market. Second, how market dominance is measured. Third, how should abuse of market dominance and avoidance of competition be dealt with.

Market dominance is the ability to set prices above the competitive level. It also refers to the ability to artificially influence the terms and conditions of trade. The factors that determine market dominance in data involve the quality and quantity of information. These are the factors that enhance market control, regardless of whether the firm in question has big data (Takagi 2020).

How to measure market dominance, and especially how to capture the market in the context of ICT developments and new market conditions, is a challenge. It is necessary to consider anti-competitiveness separately in the following cases, taking into account the various data-enabled realities of society. First, it is a contract subject to monopoly regulation. Second, it is the issue of how to consider the existence of large firms that makes it difficult for new entrants to obtain data. Finally, there is the issue of two-sided markets.

The third issue, abuse of market dominance and avoidance of competition, also poses several challenges to data privacy or infrastructure investment; however, various measures are being considered to counter them, including competition law response.

There are various possible responses to these issues of market and economic activity in the context of sophistication of society and advancement of science and technology. The main approach is to analyze markets and economic structures from

S. Hayashi and K. Arai, *Digitalization and Competition Policy in Japan*,
https://doi.org/10.1007/978-981-99-5310-3_8

the demand side. For example, market dominance has been modeled and empirically analyzed based on how firms behave to maximize their profits under the demand curve.

In contrast, the analysis of private sector corporate diversification strategies to date has been based on the supply side of the analysis. For example, Song (2015) performs a stochastic frontier analysis using financial data to estimate the multi-product distance function and estimate the efficiency index with respect to private railroad firms' diversification strategies. (The results do not show a clear relationship between the degree of diversification and efficiency.) In addition, Song (2017) estimates an inefficiency model along with technical efficiency and finds that the degree of diversification has a negative impact on efficiency, while the development of the real estate business and pure holding company system has a effect on efficiency. As a result, diversification through a systematic and manageable corporate system is suggested as a management implication. Furthermore, Song and Shoji (2016) find a small but positive relationship of the diversification index (segmental Herfindahl index) with railway investment with respect to the impact of diversification strategies on investment behavior, indicating that such strategies can be linked to revenue streams.

For diversification strategies in general, capital markets are also discounted in Japan, as confirmed by Hiramoto (2002), Tsuchimura et al. (2010), and Hanasaki and Matsushita (2014). Widening the investment opportunity gap has been pointed out to be inefficient and naïve business diversification (2010).

However, most of these analyses of business diversification have looked at the linkages and efficiencies between businesses on the supply side, and the implications of diversification from the demand side have not been seen. The principles of the economics of demand seem to suggest that firms achieve a combination of price and quantity in response to the elasticity of demand in each market. For example, using the Internet, "as the number of people who use such services to provide goods, etc. increases, the benefits to those who receive such goods, etc. are significantly increased, and this increases the number of recipients, which in turn significantly increases the benefits to the providers, which in turn further increases the number of providers." (from Article 2(1)(1) of the Law on Enhancing Transparency and Fairness of Certain Digital Platforms) Regulations for the relationships have been introduced May 27, 2020. It targets indirect network effects between multiple markets, which also requires theoretical and empirical analysis of diversification from the demand side. Therefore, this chapter examines the effects of the multisided market of private railways, which is not a digital platform, but the presence or absence of indirect network effects has not been tested so far.

New perspectives have been added to the efforts of these operators. For example, Mobility as a service (MaaS) is a service that improves people's mobility and the challenges in providing it have been examined by various operators. For example, Sakai (2019) describes MaaS initiatives in the EU and points out the importance of compatibility, interoperability and continuity. In addition, under this MaaS situation, Hörcher and Graham (2020) examines whether subscriptions are an efficient pricing tool and points out that differentiated pricing is effective. However, this has also not been examined in terms of demand-side conditions, e.g. what are the indirect network effects with other service offerings. This chapter therefore attempts to analyze the demand side conditions in this regard as well. And although the analysis of airports is where we find an analysis of the multisided marketability of demand in transport-related demand, although the analysis of airport-related projects can be found (Czerny 2013; Bracaglia et al. 2014), and in rail-related projects, we do not find anything other than Johansson et al. (2020), who looked at the relationship with employment in general. Therefore, in order to fill this gap, this chapter analyzes indirect network effects and multisided marketability in demand, with a focus on railroad-related demand.

This chapter is organized as follows. Section 2 provides a theoretical examination. In this section, in addition to the precedent analysis from a judicial perspective, an economic theoretical analysis is also carried out. Section 3 provides an empirical analysis. It examines several aspects of the indirect network effect from the demand side using data on Japanese private railways. Section 4 is the conclusion.

2 Theoretical Investigation

2.1 *Market Dominance*

In response to these problems, market dominance has traditionally used the price cost margin as an indicator of market dominance (Lerner's index), which relates to how much higher a firm is able to set its prices compared to its production costs.

In other words, a firm's profit is $P(Q)Q - C(Q)$, where $P(Q)$ is the price, Q is the quantity, $P(Q)$ is the demand function in the market, and $C(Q)$ is the total cost function. Q, which maximizes the profit, is as follows, taking the first-order condition (FOC):

$$P(Q) + P'(Q)Q - C'(Q) = 0 \tag{1}$$

If we transform this equation and let ε be the price elasticity of demand, we obtain Eq. (2):

$$\frac{P(Q) - C'(Q)}{P(Q)} = \frac{1}{\epsilon} \tag{2}$$

This means that the price cost margin (markup ratio) is inversely proportional to the price elasticity of the demand for the good.

The extended Lerner indicator in Weyl (2010), which is an extension of this indicator for multi-side platforms is instructive as the following Eq. (3),

$$\frac{P(Q)^I - \left(C'(Q)^I + \alpha N^J - \widetilde{\beta^J} N^J\right)}{P(Q)} = \frac{1}{\epsilon^I} \quad (3)$$

where $P(Q)^I$ is the price in the I market, $C'(Q)^I$ is the cost in the I market, N^J is the number of market participants in the J market, $\widetilde{\beta^J}$ is the average response of marginal customers in the J market (which represents Spence's distortion), and ϵ^I is the price elasticity in the I market.

In the debate about multi-sided platforms, it has long been argued that below-cost pricing is not indicative of predatory behavior that abuses market dominance (Evans 2003; Wright 2004). This is because it is an internal subsidy to users on one side to reflect the interests of users on the other side, and therefore does not result in an overall pricing below costs. Similarly, pricing well above cost need not be considered as an indication of significant market power. This is because if the number of users on one side interacts with users on the other side, users on the other side may be charged a higher price. Therefore, measuring market dominance in multi-sided platforms, including two-sided markets, is an old and unsolved problem in the economic analysis of competition law.

The framework of Weyl (2010) provides a simple answer to this; that it is a general Lerner index for multiple sides, which encompasses and integrates the previous Lerner indexes proposed for special models such as Armstrong (2006) and Rochet and Tirole (2006).

Such an approach is to construct them separately for each side of the market, which requires a measurement of the value of marginal user average interactions as well as costs. While this measurement may be difficult, it should not be as difficult as measuring costs. These measures can be used as a test of market dominance as well as the Lerner index. However, since prices are often close to or below zero, an index that will probably be normalized by something other than price is a more attractive measure.

With respect to this estimate, $P^I - C^I - cN^J + \tilde{b}^J N^J$ is easy to calculate. In this case, the natural test for predation in one market would be whether this is a negative number. In addition, if an overall measure of market dominance is desired, weighting in multiple markets is the natural way to aggregate. In the overall Lerner metric, intuitively, if multi-marketability (multi-sided) accounts for the bulk of profits, then we should expect relatively low prices for a given market power, since platforms tend to subsidize user participation. Thus, even if the return on sales is small, if multisided marketability (interactivity) is the main source of profit, then it will show significant market dominance. Profits are negative only if the overall Lerner index is negative.

2.2 Regulation

The regulation of multisided markets is controversial. An example is the policy debate over caps on interchange fees to card merchants and net neutrality regulations that could be variously interpreted as fees that Internet service providers (ISPs) charge for websites or impose limits on price discrimination.

Any regulation that aims to mimic the optimal benchmarks of Pigouvian and Ramsey pricing should resolve the distortions of both (Ferrari and Verboven 2012). Indeed, both pricings should resolve a certain percentage of distortions on both sides of a two-sided market, rather than just on one side, as in net neutrality and exchange fee regulation. The magnitude of these distortions suggests that two factors are important: the magnitude of classical market dominance and the distortion of Spence on the other side of the market.

Thus, the new factor in multi-sided marketability (bi-directional) is that regulators should focus most on lowering prices on the opposite side of the market from the side with greater Spence distortions. Thus, ISP regulators should focus on limiting prices in websites (net neutrality) when there is a surplus (in interactions) among loyal users in profitable websites. However, if the situation is reversed, getting ISPs to lower their prices and install more lines in consumers' homes may become a priority.

Second, implementing the regulation of Ramsey pricing requires detailed knowledge of demand that is not normally available to regulators. For this reason, it may be better to regulate only one side of the market, especially if market dominance is believed to be particularly distorting prices on one side. However, a price cap on one side of the market would lower prices on one side by either increasing the number of participants on that side by the platform operator (which the regulator requires) or reducing the number of participants on the other side (which the regulator also does not require), especially if there is a positive interaction, further, it may create distortions. Thus, according to Sheshinski (1976), price regulation tends to reduce quality. Of course, this may be desirable if the benefits of the interaction are negative, especially if Spence's distortions are upward. For example, a price cap on newspaper readers may lead to more advertising, but this may be an efficient counterbalance to market forces against advertisers, especially if average readers dislike advertising more than marginal readers, as in tabloid newspapers.

In the case of positive interaction interests and Spence distortions, Sheshinski's proposal for quantity regulation may be better, since it does not change the price incentives on the other side of the market if price regulation is not particularly attractive. Individually, the optimal pricing conditions are on the side where participation is given, and primary conditions are not affected by participation. For example, regulators may require ISPs to make a certain percentage of websites available for their services, rather than prohibiting them from charging for websites. Since a natural way to increase website participation without lowering prices is to increase the number of subscribers, this may encourage the adoption of more Internet users. Of course, in markets subject to volume regulation, care must be taken to enforce regulation to ensure that ISPs do not commit fraud by signing up for the smallest websites. Given the diversity of websites, the practical complexities of implementing such a policy may outweigh the theoretical benefits. Moreover, even at the theoretical level, a more detailed analysis is needed to clarify when participation regulation is truly preferable to price regulation and for whom it is intended, taking into account all indirect effects. Nevertheless, such allocation regulations deserve further consideration, at least in a multisided network. Empirical analysis is required to verify the necessity and sufficiency of such regulations. For this reason, in the next section, multisided network effects will be examined through empirical analysis to determine their impact.

Finally, the above analysis appears to provide a further rationale for allowing price discrimination in the two-sided market, at least when Spence distortions are positive. This is because price discrimination is usually more detrimental because it leads to higher prices for advertisers and may exacerbate market power.

3 Empirical Analysis

3.1 Previous Research

Several antitrust cases can be found, but I would like to mention three major ones here. The first was the Lorraine Journal (LJ) case (1951). LJ's exclusivity agreement with advertisers was challenged by the U.S. Department of Justice (DOJ) as a monopolizing act. In this case, the media market is the link between advertisers and users, while contracts with advertisers create barriers to entry into the media market, making the two-sided market a source of market dominance. While it is possible for any major purchaser to build barriers to entry through such contracts, in this case, it became important that it be a two-sided market.

The second was the Dallas News-Paper case (1989). The *Dallas Morning News* entered into an exclusive trade agreement with a content co-seller, specifically serialized comics. In response, the *Dallas Times Herald* filed a lawsuit claiming that this practice violated antitrust laws, which, however they lost. Newspapers are a platform for advertisers and readers, and this agreement is with a third-party supplier of quality content. As providing readers with higher quality content than their rivals, this strategy made sense regardless of how the advertising market reacted. In this case, the two-sided market was held not to be a central factor (in determining illegality) in understanding the significance of the exclusive dealing agreement.

The third was the Amex case (2016). American Express (Amex), a credit card business, prohibited the practice of encouraging customers to pay U.S. card merchants with other companies' cards, which had lower fees than Amex. The U.S. District Court in Brooklyn held that the "prohibition against inducement (evasion)" clause, which was intended to discourage customers from using other companies' cards, violated the antitrust laws. The New York Court of Appeals for the Second Circuit criticized the court for focusing solely on the merchant's benefit of using Amex for payment and not looking at the perks and benefits that cardholders could obtain, arguing that while merchants may want lower fees, the fees are necessary to keep cardholders happy. As long as the source of Amex's market share was the satisfaction of cardholders, there was no reason to intervene in the current functioning of the payment card industry, the court held. With respect to market determination, the Supreme Court held that a single market should be delineated in a way that encompasses demanders such as merchants and cardholders (holding that two-sided transaction platforms jointly supply a single commodity service), and that the anti-customer inducement clause should look not only at merchant fees, but rather at the entire credit card transaction. It had to be seen whether it was restricted or raised costs, and since these were not shown, it was held that it did not violate antitrust laws.

In addition, in the Apple APP Store case (2019), the court ruled that plaintiff standing was found when Apple used its monopoly position to set and collect unreasonable commissions for what it sells to consumers by setting app prices and setting a high commission of 30%. In terms of the economic analysis of the platform, the decision shows whether to view the two-sided nature of the platform as a single transaction is a case-by-case matter.

The empirical analysis is discussed in the following studies: "The literature on two-sided markets is developing rapidly" (Rysman 2009), the estimation of market power in the two-sided market for newspapers (Argentesi and Filistrucchi 2007), the analysis of vertical restrictions taking into account entry in the magazine market (Ferrari and Verboven 2012), the estimation of market dominance in the game industry with a two-sided market nature (Lee 2013), estimating the effects of newspaper market mergers that also take into account product characteristics (Fan 2013), analyzing differentiation under a two-sided market based on the ideological nature of newspapers (Gentzkow et al. 2014), and examining the effects of local television stations on the pricing behavior of intermediaries under the two-sided market nature of local television stations (Boik 2016). Other analyses have been conducted from a variety of perspectives. In terms of matching models, it has also been summarized that knowing the observable characteristics of partners may not be enough to estimate the parameters sought (Chiappori and Salanié 2016).

With respect to the economic analysis of the two-sided market in Japan, Doi (2017) provides a qualitative analysis of the gaming industry, Kawai (2019) provides a qualitative analysis of cross-platform strategies, and Kadota (2019) provides a qualitative analysis of Amazon's pricing strategy. In terms of quantitative analysis, Sunada and Ohashi (2010) estimated the demand functions of the reader and advertiser sides using magazines as the subject matter. He compared models on whether the Japanese magazine market is competitive or cooperative, and found that both readers and advertisers are competitive. Although there was no estimation of market dominance, the average margin rate was 9.3% (median 18.3%) for readers and 35.0% (median 34.8%) for advertisers, suggesting that the influence of the readers' side was greater than that of the advertisers' side. In addition, Kuroda (2010) analyzed content delivery platforms using mobile phone operators as a two-sided market between mobile phone users and content providers. The results show that subsidies are given from subscribers to content providers, and the policy to promote competition is discussed.

3.2 *Necessity and Sufficiency of Railway Business Research*

This chapter attempts to estimate the market dominance of the two-sided market using segmental financial information in the railroad business. In some respects, the two-sided marketability in the railroad business is similar to that in the magazine and newspaper business, but it is not intuitively clear whether customer growth is directly related to the profitability of the other businesses. This chapter examines the general view that an increase in customers in the market for transportation services as a way to ensure the footfall of residents along the line leads to growth in other markets, such as the growth of residents' leisure services, the expansion of real estate transactions along the line, and an increase in customers in the retail and other distribution businesses for residents along the line. It considers the potential for indirect network effects outside the market, such as the impact of increased sales from the rail business on market expansion in other businesses (e.g., leisure and services, real estate, distribution, etc.), not only through direct prices, but also through the impact of increased customers. This would appropriately satisfy the need for empirical research to understand indirect network effects beyond the inherent need for rail business research.

This segmental information on the railway business to be studied provides an example of how to understand market dominance in a new industry, including platforms, which is the objective of this chapter, whose methodology and results are considered to be a sufficient contribution to digital market research. The segment information under consideration here is disclosed in such a way that it provides appropriate information about the various business activities undertaken by an entity and the operating environment in which the entity operates, so that users of financial statements can understand the entity's past performance and properly evaluate forecasts of future cash flows (Accounting Standards Board of Japan 2010). Business segments are (1) those related to business activities that earn revenue and incur expenses; (2) those for which the entity's chief operating decision-making body makes decisions about the resources to be allocated to the component unit and periodically registers its operating results for the purpose of evaluating its performance, and (3) those for which discrete financial information is available. It is considered applicable to all.

The use of segmental information in this chapter is based on the following three points. First, it allows us to analyze business behavior more appropriately by looking directly at the decision-making criteria for business behavior; second, it allows us to look at both the industry of natural monopoly and other business markets for each individual business in terms of the competitive situation in each competing market. This is because the data is believed to allow for the identification of the two-sided marketability of the transportation business and other businesses. The third point is as follows: although the Amex case decision was considered to be a joint transaction, it was believed that the two-sided marketability would be more clearly identified between the transportation business and other businesses.

3.3 Data and Models

The data for the 11 major railroad companies in the Nikkei NEEDS Financial Quest are as follows: (1) Transportation (Transportation revenue: ts, Transportation profit: tp); (2) Leisure Services revenue: ls, Leisure Services profit: lp), (3) Real Estate (sales of the real estate business: es, profit of the real estate business: ep), and (4) distribution business (sales of the distribution business: rs, profit of the distribution business: rp). These figures are common to all the major railway companies (except Odakyu Electric Railway, which does not have leisure and service operations), and to some of the other companies. In addition, some other companies have indicated that they are in the construction business, but these are not included here.

The transportation business is shared by all the companies and includes the railway business and the bus and taxi businesses, which are the core businesses of the companies under consideration. With the exception of the Odakyu Electric Railway, the Leisure and Service segment includes amusement parks, sightseeing, sports facilities, and hotels. The Real Estate segment is common to all companies, and includes real estate subdivisions and real estate leasing. The distribution business includes department stores and retail store businesses (Moriya 2002).

The descriptive statistics for the data used are shown in Table 1.

All of the companies are primarily involved in the railway business, but there are a few companies with larger distribution businesses, such as Keio Dentetsu, Kintetsu Group, Keihan Holdings, and Odakyu Electric Railway, and a few companies with larger leisure and service businesses, such as the Kintetsu Group.

First, we check whether the transportation business, which is the core business of each company, is two-sided in relation to the other businesses. As a method to examine the indirect network effect, we confirm that β4.1 in the following equation using Eq. (4) is positive and significant, as is the coefficient on the sales of the transportation business.

$$\begin{aligned} &\text{ReturnOnSales}_{\text{RelatedSegment}} = \text{Constant}(C)_{\text{RelatedSegment}} \\ &+ \beta_{4,1}\text{Sales}_{\text{TransportationBbusinessSegment}} \\ &\left(+\beta_{4,2}\text{Sales}_{\text{RelatedSegment}} + \beta_{4,3}\left(\text{Sales}_{\text{RelatedSegment}}\right)^2\right) \\ &+ \text{firm fixed effects} + \text{time fixed effects} + \varepsilon_4 \end{aligned} \tag{4}$$

This is estimated for the leisure and services, real estate, and distribution businesses. The data are from the fiscal year ended March 2010 to the fiscal year ended December 2019.

Table 1 Descriptive statistics

	Tobu Railway	Tokyu	Keikyu	Keio	Keisei Electric Railway	Nishi-Nippon Railroad	Kintetsu Group Holdings	Nankai Electric Railway	Keihan holdings	Nagoya railroad	Odakyu electric railway
TS mean	133,384.1	123,549.8	74,401.3	80,469.0	87,043.6	53,933.3	139,241.1	58,247.3	57,923.4	105,030.2	107,891.2
TS median	131,964.5	122,792.0	74,396.0	80,559.5	87,317.0	54,114.0	137,901.5	57,736.0	58,174.0	102,024.0	107,799.0
TS maximum	217,107.0	213,602.0	124,748.0	132,224.0	154,004.0	92,175.0	231,989.0	102,051.0	94,605.0	298,865.0	179,293.0
TS minimum	49,353.0	45,061.0	27,610.0	30,867.0	30,356.0	20,653.0	52,688.0	20,704.0	22,788.0	38,425.0	39,782.0
TS std. dev	60,175.9	56,657.9	33,515.5	36,136.0	39,484.4	24,505.4	63,137.7	26,667.4	25,746.0	54,713.1	48,415.8
TP mean	21,419.1	19,713.6	11,397.7	10,181.3	13,005.5	3392.5	19,794.4	9001.9	6306.6	12,498.4	19,790.3
TP median	20,651.0	19,141.0	11,724.0	10,675.0	13,755.0	3245.5	20,569.5	9149.5	6209.5	12,605.5	20,130.0
TP maximum	41,167.0	29,498.0	21,550.0	15,656.0	22,448.0	7251.0	32,943.0	16,500.0	11,630.0	24,379.0	29,795.0
TP minimum	5882.0	7628.0	2509.0	4366.0	3352.0	997.0	6507.0	2864.0	2401.0	2976.0	7140.0
TP std. dev	10,051.6	7423.1	5261.7	3522.2	5440.7	1691.1	8237.9	3903.1	2516.9	6139.4	7310.7
LS mean	45,988.3	59,764.4	24,683.8	44,092.2	6319.0	24,444.7	243,581.8	22,249.9	18,408.5	35,978.6	–
LS median	41,701.5	58,408.0	23,842.0	42,854.0	6438.0	24,287.0	230,539.0	22,393.5	17,966.5	33,891.5	–
LS maximum	79,991.0	105,502.0	44,202.0	80,477.0	11,916.0	45,696.0	500,475.0	39,640.0	36,538.0	140,189.0	–
LS minimum	12,752.0	18,438.0	8025.0	12,691.0	2153.0	7963.0	38,417.0	7696.0	5551.0	12,159.0	–

(continued)

Table 1 (continued)

	Tobu Railway	Tokyu	Keikyu	Keio	Keisei Electric Railway	Nishi-Nippon Railroad	Kintetsu Group Holdings	Nankai Electric Railway	Keihan holdings	Nagoya railroad	Odakyu electric railway
LS std. dev	22,176.6	27,678.4	11,710.4	20,806.1	3078.5	11,643.7	140,197.5	10,689.8	8780.8	22,941.2	–
LP mean	3479.2	1852.0	2434.2	3628.5	77.0	799.7	3622.1	900.3	1847.4	651.7	–
LP median	2891.5	1660.0	2446.5	3389.5	59.0	921.0	3084.0	669.0	1244.0	802.5	–
LP maximum	12,077.0	6664.0	6343.0	7206.0	341.0	2295.0	10,562.0	2388.0	5009.0	2102.0	–
LP minimum	– 1303.0	– 2282.0	– 1650.0	– 176.0	– 247.0	– 1346.0	– 2844.0	177.0	– 857.0	– 1500.0	–
LP std. dev	3424.5	2278.6	2164.4	1967.6	136.1	862.9	3626.3	592.7	1577.0	872.4	–
ES mean	34,347.8	110,116.9	22,260.9	21,722.9	12,158.8	33,962.2	82,416.1	18,962.3	47,854.4	48,960.8	37,208.9
ES median	34,194.5	104,394.0	18,617.5	19,830.5	12,102.5	31,357.5	73,098.0	17,721.5	40,587.0	44,742.5	34,099.5
ES maximum	63,867.0	203,363.0	69,927.0	50,004.0	22,486.0	88,201.0	164,245.0	41,248.0	118,607.0	96,492.0	73,002.0
ES minimum	10,465.0	36,609.0	4374.0	6388.0	3498.0	10,696.0	19,991.0	5039.0	9060.0	12,712.0	11,758.0
ES std. dev	16,827.2	52,537.9	14,772.2	11,423.4	6199.3	19,142.1	45,829.9	9871.6	28,717.0	27,289.0	19,905.0
EP mean	6311.3	18,292.2	1274.3	6099.6	3205.3	4848.8	7367.0	5462.6	8043.0	5138.2	6884.3
EP median	5941.0	16,658.5	1113.5	6226.5	2958.5	4458.5	7663.0	5182.0	7298.5	4577.0	6439.0
EP maximum	14,394.0	32,357.0	8449.0	10,251.0	6773.0	10,489.0	18,698.0	11,402.0	17,468.0	11,955.0	13,759.0

(continued)

Table 1 (continued)

	Tobu Railway	Tokyu	Keikyu	Keio	Keisei Electric Railway	Nishi-Nippon Railroad	Kintetsu Group Holdings	Nankai Electric Railway	Keihan holdings	Nagoya railroad	Odakyu electric railway
EP minimum	1083.0	5428.0	– 17,647.0	2273.0	864.0	1130.0	– 462.0	1695.0	1677.0	– 777.0	1327.0
EP std. dev	3827.7	7970.8	3696.6	2586.2	1850.2	2791.0	5144.9	2609.0	4221.4	3321.5	3582.3
RS mean	128,420.5	376,281.1	67,639.3	101,162.2	44,145.4	48,511.3	241,374.0	19,065.4	60,572.8	84,725.9	137,499.7
RS median	136,851.0	363,232.0	71,045.5	99,578.5	43,655.0	45,660.5	238,327.0	17,883.0	60,046.5	71,510.5	133,737.5
RS maximum	228,161.0	703,183.0	120,874.0	172,455.0	75,961.0	81,796.0	408,697.0	35,794.0	100,709.0	149,997.0	232,648.0
RS minimum	46,477.0	122,433.0	24,629.0	38,367.0	17,151.0	17,360.0	89,963.0	5791.0	22,742.0	31,719.0	52,207.0
RS std. dev	59,820.9	179,012.6	31,081.1	46,872.9	20,204.8	22,382.1	111,604.4	9166.9	28,120.6	39,881.1	63,179.6
RP mean	748.0	6694.1	1072.6	3287.4	586.8	589.9	2571.0	1930.5	1543.0	499.3	2196.5
RP median	584.0	5830.5	985.5	3203.5	522.0	320.0	1929.0	1749.5	1408.0	370.5	2027.0
RP maximum	2292.0	17,139.0	2622.0	5327.0	1270.0	8180.0	7783.0	4011.0	3161.0	2585.0	4647.0
RP minimum	– 536.0	1236.0	– 36.0	1383.0	115.0	– 101.0	– 1045.0	526.0	505.0	– 684.0	502.0
RP std. dev	758.5	4082.6	730.8	1366.1	297.8	1279.3	1907.9	997.3	821.8	679.3	979.2

3.4 Estimation Results

The results show that the coefficient of determination, adjusted for degrees of freedom, generally dampens from 0.7 to 0.8, explaining about 70–80% of the variation. In terms of the relationship between each business and the transportation business, the increase in sales of the transportation business has a positive effect on the leisure and services business (row 2: the values of ts. Positive indirect network effect). We do not find a significant relationship between real estate and distribution businesses. Considering the effect of the size of sales of each business itself and its square effect, the distribution business also has a positive effect. There is a possibility of the reverse causality that success of leisure or real estate division increases profit of transportation division.

The results are shown in Table 2.

The symbols have the same meaning as those in the following tables.

Similarly, the relationship between these four businesses is estimated using the following Eq. (5), as shown in Table 3. It looks at the relationship between the increase in sales of each business and the increase in the target's operating margin of sales.

$$\begin{aligned}\text{ReturnOnSales}_{\text{RelatedSegment}} &= \text{Constant}(C)_{\text{RelatedSegment}} \\ &+ \sum \beta_{5,1}\text{Sales}_{\text{OtherThanRelatedSegment}} \\ &\left(+\beta_{5,2}\text{Sales}_{\text{RelatedSegment}}\right) \\ &+ \text{firm fixed effects} + \text{time fixed effects } \varepsilon_5 \end{aligned} \tag{5}$$

According to the results, excluding or adding the sales of the business in question does not make a significant difference to the adjusted coefficient of determination, both of which explain between 70 and 80% of the total variation. As a result of the two-sided nature of the results, the profit margin of the transportation business increases when sales of the real estate business increase, and decreases when sales of the leisure services and distribution businesses increase. The profit margin of the leisure services business increases when sales of the transportation business increase, and the profit margin of the real estate business increases when sales of the leisure services and distribution businesses increase. The profit margin of the real estate business will increase with an increase in sales of the leisure service business. The profit margin of the distribution business will increase when sales of the real estate business increase. Profit margins are about 17% on average for the real estate business and about 14% on average for the railroad business, while those of the leisure services and distribution businesses are about 1–2% each.

In other words, it is possible that the transportation business may subsidize the leisure services and distribution businesses internally (profits in the transportation business would be higher if the leisure services and distribution businesses are a bit smaller), and that the positive effect of the leisure services and distribution businesses on the real estate business may be one of the reasons for this outcome.

Table 2 Two-sided marketability

Dependent Variable:	lp/ls		ep/es		rp/rs		lp/ls	
Observations	n = 399		n = 440		n = 440		n = 399	
Method: pooles least squares	Coefficient		Coefficient		Coefficient		Coefficient	
	(Std. error)		(Std. error)		(Std. error)		(Std. error)	
C	0.030	***	0.161	***	0.019	***	0.025	***
	(0.0092)		(0.0157)		(0.0033)		(0.0097)	
ts	2.02E−07	**	2.18E−07		4.73E−08		4.74E−07	***
	(9.94E−08)		(1.67E−07)		(3.46E−08)		(1.18E−07)	
ls							− 4.77E−07	***
							(1.66E−07)	
ls^2							5.25E−13	**
							(2.65E−13)	
es								
es^2								
rs								
rs^2								
Firm effects	Yes		Yes		Yes		Yes	
Period effects	Yes		Yes		Yes		Yes	
R-squared	0.727		0.726		0.868		0.740	

(continued)

Table 2 (continued)

Dependent Variable:	lp/ls		ep/es		rp/rs		lp/ls	
Observations	n = 399		n = 440		n = 440		n = 399	
Method: pooles least squares	Coefficient		Coefficient		Coefficient		Coefficient	
	(Std. error)		(Std. error)		(Std. error)		(Std. error)	
Adjusted R-squared	0.689		0.691		0.852		0.702	
S.E. of regression	0.031		0.052		0.011		0.030	
Akaike info criterion	− 4.004		− 2.957		− 6.101		− 4.043	
Dependent variable:	ep/es		rp/rs		ep/es		rp/rs	
Observations	n = 440		n = 440		n = 440		n = 440	
Method: pooles least squares	Coefficient		Coefficient		Coefficient		Coefficient	
	(Std. error)		(Std. error)		(Std. error)		(Std. error)	
C	0.166	***	0.020	***	0.166	***	0.020	***
	(0.0209)		(0.0038)		(0.0209)		(0.0038)	
ts	1.90E−07		9.36E−08	**	1.90E−07		9.36E−08	**
	(1.90E−07)		(4.56E−08)		(1.90E−07)		(4.56E−08)	
ls								
ls^2								
es	− 1.12E−07				− 1.12E−07			
	(4.69E−07)				(4.69E−07)			

(continued)

Table 2 (continued)

Dependent variable:	ep/es		rp/rs		ep/es		rp/rs	
Observations	n = 440		n = 440		n = 440		n = 440	
Method: pooles least squares	Coefficient		Coefficient		Coefficient		Coefficient	
	(Std. error)		(Std. error)		(Std. error)		(Std. error)	
es^2	6.92E−13				6.92E−13			
	(1.90E−12)				(1.90E−12)			
rs			− 5.96E−08				− 5.96E−08	
			(3.87E−08)				(3.87E−08)	
rs^2			5.16E−14				5.16E−14	
			(4.20E−14)				(4.20E−14)	
Firm effects	Yes		Yes		Yes		Yes	
Period effects	Yes		Yes		Yes		Yes	
Adjusted R-squared	0.726		0.869		0.726		0.869	
	0.689		0.852		0.689		0.852	
S.E. of regression	0.052		0.011		0.052		0.011	
Akaike info criterion	− 2.948		− 6.099		− 2.948		− 6.099	

Notes The upper values in the cell are estimated coefficients and the lower values in the parenthesis are standard errors
***Significant at the 1% level
**Significant at the 5% level
*Significant at the 10% level

Table 3 Two-sidedness interrelationships between markets

Dependent variable	tp/ts		tp/ts		lp/ls		lp/ls	
Observations	n = 400		n = 400		n = 399		n = 399	
Method: pooles least squares	Coefficient		Coefficient		Coefficient		Coefficient	
	(Std. error)		(Std. error)		(Std. error)		(Std. error)	
C	0.145	***	0.137	**	0.025	**	0.011	
	(0.003)		(0.006)		(0.010)		(0.010)	
TS			1.19E−07		2.89E−07	**	4.94E−07	***
			(7.94E−08)		(1.25E−07)		(1.32E−07)	
LS	− 5.36E−08	**	− 6.97E−08	**			− 1.97E−07	***
	(2.66E−08)		(2.86E−08)				(4.74E−08)	
ES	1.99E−07	**	2.14E−07	**	1.47E−07		3.85E−07	**
	(9.88E−08)		(9.91E−08)		(1.57E−07)		(1.64E−07)	
RS	− 9.92E−08	***	− 1.21E−07	***	− 8.15E−08		− 1.24E−07	**
	(2.90E−08)		(3.24E−08)		(5.39E−08)		(5.36E−08)	
Firm effects	Yes		Yes		Yes		Yes	
Period effects	Yes		Yes		Yes		Yes	
R-squared	0.831		0.832		0.729		0.742	
Adjusted R-squared	0.806		0.806		0.689		0.703	
S.E. of regression	0.018		0.018		0.031		0.030	
Akaike info criterion	− 5.052		− 5.053		− 4.001		− 4.044	

(continued)

Table 3 (continued)

Dependent variable	ep/es		ep/es		rp/rs		rp/rs	
Observations	n = 400		n = 400		n = 400		n = 400	
Method: pooles least squares	Coefficient		Coefficient		Coefficient		Coefficient	
	(Std. error)		(Std. error)		(Std. error)		(Std. error)	
C	0.172	***	0.173	***	0.019	***	0.012	***
	(0.017)		(0.018)		(0.003)		(0.004)	
TS	1.75E−08		9.06E−09		1.39E−09		1.08E−07	**
	(2.33E−07)		(2.35E−07)		(4.35E−08)		(4.70E−08)	
LS	1.82E−07	**	1.92E−07	**	− 1.88E−08		− 3.53E−08	***
	(7.93E−08)		(8.48E−08)		(1.72E−08)		(1.69E−08)	
ES			− 1.01E−07		1.46E−07	***	3.58E−07	***
			(2.94E−07)		(4.30E−08)		(5.87E−08)	
RS	− 1.72E−08		6.06E−09				− 9.78E−08	***
	(6.77E−08)		(9.59E−08)				(1.92E−08)	
Firm effects	Yes		Yes		Yes		Yes	
Period effects	Yes		Yes		Yes		Yes	
R-squared	0.738		0.738		0.738		0.883	
Adjusted R-squared	0.699		0.698		0.699		0.866	
S.E. of regression	0.054		0.054		0.054		0.011	
Akaike info criterion	− 2.887		− 2.882		− 2.887		− 6.101	

Table 4 shows the results of the modified Lerner index of market dominance for the transportation business, often referred to as the so-called natural monopoly industry for each company.

Next, we examine whether a positive indirect network effect on the two-sided market occurs through a difference-in-difference test. Specifically, we consider a disruption in Tobu Railway and Tokyu on March 16, 2013, when the Tobu-Tojo Line started interconnecting with the Tokyu Toyoko Line via the Tokyo Metro Fukutoshin Line during the period under study (see Fig. 1). This event is added as a dummy variable (IC) in the case of Tobu Railway and Tokyu (a variable that takes 1 after the start of interconnections and 0 otherwise). We attempt to test the effect of interconnections (i.e., if there is a positive effect, we assume that the expansion of transit passengers has some kind of an indirect network effect) by using the coefficient in this IC term. The estimated equation is Eq. (5) plus the IC term.

The results are shown in Table 5.

According to the results, the results are interpreted as explaining 70–80% of the adjusted determination coefficients, which have a certain explanatory power. The noteworthy effect of cross-routing was strongly and significantly positive, especially in the real estate business. The transportation business had a weak and significantly negative effect, while the leisure service business had a weak and significantly positive effect. The results indicate that the transportation business itself was not positively affected by cross-transportation, but the real estate business and the leisure service business, which have two-sided market characteristics, were positively affected by cross-transportation.

Table 4 Adjusted Lerner index of the transport business for each company

	Adjusted Lerner index (%)
Tobu Railway	17.4
Tokyu	18.8
Keikyu	16.0
Keio	14.5
Keisei Electric Railway	15.7
Nishi-Nippon Railroad	6.4
Kintetsu Group Holdings	16.7
Nankai Electric Railway	15.8
Keihan Holdings	11.5
Nagoya Railroad	12.6

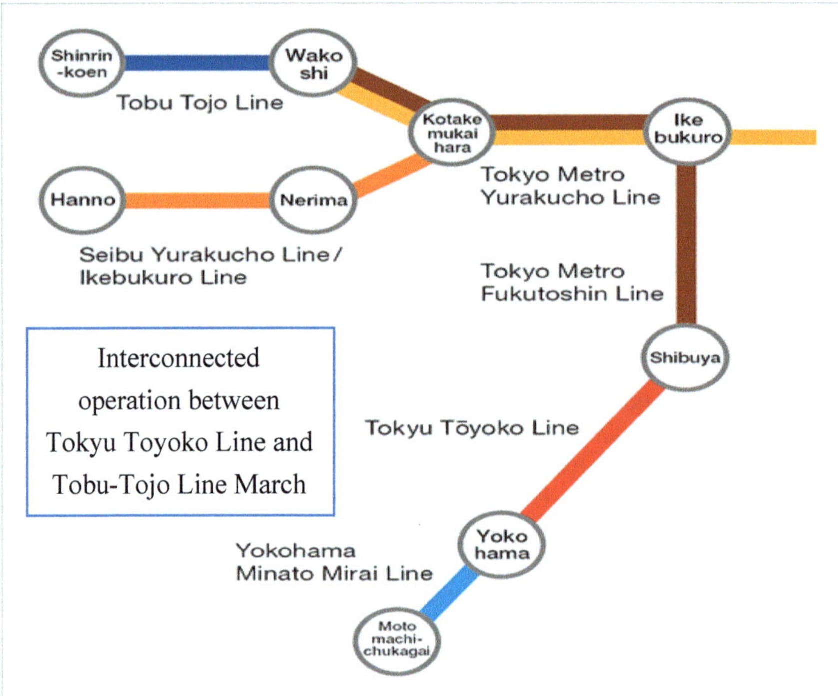

Fig. 1 Tobu-Tokyu interconnection. From the Tokyu website

3.5 Empirical Analysis Results

This section of the empirical analysis examines the two-sided marketability between segments in the rail business and confirms the potential for internal subsidies of the transportation business to the leisure and service business and the distribution business as well as the fact that the real estate business has a particularly strong indirect network effect with the transportation business, not only in the panel analysis, but also in the difference-in-differences analysis. From the point of view of preventing the abuse of market dominance, these results should be utilized in the future as background information that needs to be examined in more detail when some questionable activities occur.

Table 5 Verification of the two-sidedness difference in difference testing

Dependent Variable:	tp/ts		lp/ls		ep/es		rp/rs	
Observations	n = 400		n = 399		n = 400		n = 400	
Method: pooles least squares	Coefficient		Coefficient		Coefficient		Coefficient	
	(Std. error)		(Std. error)		(Std. error)		(Std. error)	
C	0.139	***	0.009		0.164	***	0.012	***
	(0.006)		(0.010)		(0.018)		(0.004)	
TS	1.15E–07		5.01E–07	***	3.76E–08		1.10E–07	**
	(7.92E–08)		(1.31E–07)		(2.31E–07)		(4.70E–08)	
LS	– 7.24E–08	**	– 1.92E–07	***	2.10E–07	**	– 3.42E–08	**
	(2.86E–08)		(4.73E–08)		(8.33E–08)		(1.70E–08)	
ES	1.94E–07	*	4.20E–07	**	3.44E–08		3.66E–07	***
	(9.96E–08)		(1.65E–07)		(2.90E–07)		(5.91E–08)	
RS	– 1.11E–07	***	– 1.41E–07	**	– 5.94E–08		– 1.02E–07	***
	(3.28E–08)		(5.43E–08)		(9.56E–08)		(1.95E–08)	
Interconnect	– 0.008	*	0.014	*	0.055	***	0.003	
	(0.005)		(0.008)		(0.014)		(0.003)	
Firm effects	Yes		Yes		Yes		Yes	
Period effects	Yes		Yes		Yes		Yes	
R-squared	0.833		0.744		0.748		0.884	
Adjusted R-squared	0.807		0.705		0.710		0.866	
S.E. of regression	0.018		0.030		0.053		0.011	
Akaike info criterion	– 5.056		– 4.048		– 2.919		– 6.100	

4 Conclusion

In this chapter, as a concrete example of the verification, we conducted an empirical analysis of two-sided marketability based on segmental financial data, including the aspect on whether the increase in sales of the transportation business raises the profit margin of the real estate business for railway companies. The results show that there is a two-sidedness among many businesses. The effects were found to be both positive indirect network effects and negative ones (such as too much advertising leading to fewer subscribers, so to speak). By examining the differences based on the startup events of the crossover, we find that the indirect network effect in the transportation business is demonstrated to a certain extent, and that its manifestation is not uniform across businesses, with some businesses showing strong effects and others showing less visible effects. Although we also estimate market dominance using an actual modified Lerner index, we do not estimate Spence's distortions in this chapter, and we may need to further improve the accuracy of our estimates when discussing actual policy.

There are three management implications of this chapter. First, in business diversification, it is easy to be blinded by supply side efficiency, including the economics of scope. However, there is a need for strategic policy formulation from the demand side, such as the presence or absence of indirect network effects that go beyond simply considering prices and volumes in response to differences in the elasticity of demand in different markets. Second, indirect network effects may also, however, have a negative effect, and therefore careful policy formulation based on empirical analysis, such as social experiments and data processing, is needed in the actual development of the project, even from a tactical perspective. Third, the analysis of the multisided market among the segments of private railways, in particular, confirms the results of previous research on business diversification (e.g., the development of the real estate business has a positive impact on efficiency), since the transportation business has an indirect network effect on the leisure and service business and the distribution business. Further elaboration may be needed on how the decline in profit margins may be due to segment characteristics that are separate from business strategy.

The policy implication of this chapter is that the manifestations of indirect network effects are not uniform for operators operating in multisided markets, and it is important to look at ensuring appropriate competition on a case-by-case basis. One of the limitations and challenges of this chapter is that it is a case study of a large private railway company. However, the methodology in this chapter, which analyzes companies and industries that have traditionally been analyzed from the perspective of business diversification from a demand perspective, has great potential for application beyond case studies. In this sense, we need to expand the scope of our analysis to include digital platforms, which have become a challenge today, and promote further empirical research.

5 Summary

In this chapter, we examine multiple segments, conventionally analyzed from the perspective of business diversification, from multiple perspectives in a multisided market. Specifically, based on segmental financial data, we conduct an empirical analysis of whether increased sales in the transportation business increase the profit margin of the real estate business of a railroad company. The results show that there are two types of sidedness among many businesses. The effects of both positive and negative indirect network effects were found to exist. In addition, verification of the difference-in-differences based on the initiation event of the mutual traffic interconnection demonstrates the indirect network effect in the transportation business to a certain extent, and shows that the effect is not uniform in each business, with some businesses showing strong effects and others showing less visible effects.

References

Accounting Standards Board of Japan (2010) Corporate Accounting Standard No. 17. The Accounting Standard for disclosures about segments of an enterprise and related information, and Corporate Accounting Standard Implementation Guidance No. 20, the guidance on accounting standard for disclosures about segments of an enterprise and related information. https://www.asb.or.jp/jp/accounting_standards/accounting_standards/y2008/2008-0321.html

Argentesi E, Filistrucchi L (2007) Estimating market power in a two-sided market: the case of newspapers. J Appl Econ 22(7):1247–1266

Armstrong M (2006) Competition in two-sided markets. RAND J Econ 37(3):668–691

Boik A (2016) Intermediaries in two-sided markets: an empirical analysis of the US cable television industry. Am Econ J: Microecon 8(1):256–282

Bracaglia V, Alfonso TD, Nastasi A (2014) Competition between multiproduct airports. Econ Transp 3(4):270–281

Chiappori P-A, Salanié B (2016) The econometrics of matching models. J Econ Lit 54(3):832–861

Czerny AI (2013) Public versus private airport behavior when concession revenues exist. Econ Transp 2(1):38–46

Doi N (2017) Business models and competition in a two-sided market: a country examples of the gaming industry. J Econ 71(3):43–58 in Japanese

Evans DS (2003) Some empirical aspects of multi-sided platform industries. Rev Netw Econ 2(3):191–209

Fan Y (2013) Ownership consolidation and product characteristics: a study of the US daily newspaper market. Am Econ Rev 103(5):1598–1628

Ferrari S, Verboven F (2012) Vertical control of a distribution network-an empirical analysis of magazines. RAND J Econ 43(1):26–50

Gentzkow M, Shapiro JM, Sinkinson M (2014) Competition and ideological diversity: historical evidence from US newspapers. Am Econ Rev 104(10):3073–3114

Hanasaki M, Matsushita K (2014) Corporate governance and diversified behavior: an empirical analysis using Japanese corporate data. J Econ Bus Res 34(5):1–74 in Japanese

Hiramoto T (2002) Business diversification and corporate value. Gendai Finance 12:31–55 in Japanese

Hörcher D, Graham DJ (2020) MaaS economics: should we fight car ownership with subscriptions to alternative modes? Econ Transp 22:100167. https://doi.org/10.1016/j.ecotra.2020.100167

Johansson E, Camporeale R, Palmqvist C-W (2020) Railway network design and regional labour markets in Sweden. Res Transp Econ 100921. Available online https://doi.org/10.1016/j.retrec.2020.100921

Kadota Y (2019) Pricing strategies for platforms in the two-way market and cost sharing: a case study of Amazon's online shopping. J Commun 66(4):23–50 in Japanese

Kawai T (2019) A tentative framework of dynamic platform strategy—for the era of GAFA and 5G. J Strateg Manage Stud 11(1):19–36

Kuroda T (2010) An analysis of the price structure of mobile phone content delivery platforms using a two-sided market model. J Tokyo Keizai Univ 267:171–189 in Japanese

Lee RS (2013) Vertical integration and exclusivity in platform and two-sided markets. Am Econ Rev 103(7):2960–3000

Moriya H (2002) The 15 largest private railway companies and their profit and loss structures: trends by consolidated and unconsolidated companies and business segment. J Inst Res Econ Culture 7:79–105 in Japanese
Rochet J-C, Tirole J (2006) Two-sided markets: a progress report. RAND J Econ 37(3):645–667
Rysman M (2009) The economics of two-sided markets. J Econ Perspect 23(3):125–143
Sakai K (2019) MaaS trends and policy-level initiatives in the EU. IATSS Res 43(4):207–209
Sheshinski E (1976) Price, quality and quantity regulation in monopoly situations. Economica 43(17):127–137
Song J (2015) Considerations on the impact and efficiency of diversification strategies in Japanese private railway companies. J Transp Stud 58:49–56 in Japanese
Song J (2017) An empirical analysis of diversified business development and efficiency in Japanese private railway enterprises. J Transp Stud 60:31–38 in Japanese
Song J, Shoji K (2016) The impact of diversification strategies of major private railways on investment behavior. Natl Econ J 213(5):17–31 in Japanese
Sunada M, Ohashi H (2010) Economic analysis of the two-sided market. CPRC Joint Research Report CR-0210, in Japanese
Takagi S (2020) Literature survey on the economic impact of digital platforms. Int J Econ Policy Stud 14:449–464
Tsuchimura N, Sugiura Y, Sasaki T, Yonezawa Y (2010) Diversification and the role of internal capital markets in Japanese firms. Gendai Finance 27:41–57 in Japanese
Weyl EG (2010) A price theory of multi-sided platforms. Am Econ Rev 100(4):1642–1672
Wright J (2004) One-sided logic in two-sided markets. Rev Netw Econ 3(1):44–64

Chapter 9
Competition Law and Consumers in Digital Platforms

1 Introduction

In the digital market, giant platform (PF) providers, represented by global players such as GAFA, are expanding their market position through the use of big data obtained from consumers. Since digital platform (DPF) firms are characterized by their tendency to monopolize or oligopolize the market, there has been an increasing number of competition law violations by DPF operators, the development of various legal systems, and academic discussions with the aim of protecting consumer rights and ensuring transparency and fairness in the trading environment.

In light of this current state of the digital market, this chapter describes discussions on information fiduciary (including academic theories and foreign legislations), necessity of clarifying "consumer rights", and importance of "trust" behind it. We summarize in this chapter the Antimonopoly Act (regulation on abuse of superior bargaining position), and the Digital Platform Transparency Act. In addition to this, we analyze the applicability of the Act against Unjustifiable Premiums and Misleading Representations (the November 25, 2019 ruling of the Tokyo District Court in the case of Amazon Japan's request for revocation of a cease-and-desist order[1]), the vicarious liability of online platform firms (Chujitsuya case[2]), and the liability for DPF system construction (Yahoo! Auction case).

From the perspective of competition law, we consider it necessary and appropriate to impose information fiduciary duty on DPFs in view of the realities of the digital market. Reasons why DPF should be subject to the information fiduciary duty are as follows:

---

[1] https://www.courts.go.jp%2Fapp%2Ffiles%2Fhanrei_jp%2F404%2F089404_hanrei.pdf&usg=AOvVaw0oh8TgrxetI0UCWQAu0Z9D.

[2] Supreme Court decision of November 30, 1995, Minshu Vol. 49, No. 9, p. 2972: https://www.courts.go.jp/app/hanrei_jp/detail2?id=57055e.

S. Hayashi and K. Arai, *Digitalization and Competition Policy in Japan*,
https://doi.org/10.1007/978-981-99-5310-3_9

The first reason is the asymmetry in status and information between DPF operators and consumers. The asymmetry of information between DPF operators and consumers is huge, and the position of consumers compared to DPF operators is extremely vulnerable. While it is extremely difficult for individual consumers to monitor the behavior of DPF operators and prevent DPF operators from acting in a way that harms their own interests or otherwise betrays their trust, it is easy for DPF operators to collect a wealth of information about consumers and thereby reveal consumer behavior at their will. With this as a backdrop, trust in PF services is becoming increasingly important.

The second reason is consumers' relative dependence on DPF. DPF provides a variety of services that consumers need, and since they have no choice but to use the services they need, they have no choice but to trust the actions of DPF.

The third reason is that DPF operators behave as professional service providers who collect and use data. DPF operators are now providing information infrastructure that is indispensable for consumers (individuals) and businesses in the social economy. In fact, the political and economic situation in the United States is fresh in our minds. Nowadays, the provision of information infrastructure is one of the infrastructures of society. As a background to discipline by competition law, various restrictions on DPF operators with market dominance may be necessary.

The fourth reason is importance of trust in DPF operators. There is a widespread social demand for DPF to behave as a trustworthy organization that acts in a manner consistent with the interests of consumers, regardless of whether it pursues profits.

In discussions about information fiduciary, it is essential to consider the economic perspective. The economic characteristics of goods are examined from an economic perspective on the information treated in this chapter. The examination depends on the content of the information, but in the case of personal information, which is the subject of discussion, it is highly likely that personal information has an external economy (those who utilize personal information are likely to create added value as the information increases). Because of the irreversible nature of goods, moral hazard (inefficiency resulting from the inability to control behavior after knowing) and adverse selection (suppression of transactions and markets because the quality cannot be confirmed before knowing) may occur. Given these characteristics, there may be areas that fall outside the discipline of normal market transactions.

For this reason, even if the ownership of information is transferred, certain rights and obligations are set by contract.[3] This has been disciplined as a trust in the past. The idea here is to apply this to DPFs that handle information.

In terms of economics, the idea is to provide a certain direction for smooth transactions and market formation based on the characteristics of goods. To give an example, in the case of education and intellectual property, which have external economies, the government is involved. Another example is that there are prudential regulations and certain other disciplines for the behavior of financial institutions that are prone to moral hazard. Also, the insurance market, which is prone to adverse selection, has compulsory insurance and other systems.

[3] See the JFTC's Intellectual Property Guidelines: https://www.jftc.go.jp/en/legislation_gls/imonopoly_guidelines_files/IPGL_Frand.pdf.

In terms of tackling digital oligopoly, researches have focused on active enforcement actions against collusive practices (Jedlicková 2019) and introduction of GDPR-like disclosure requirements for framing algorithms (Loderer and Picht 2019). In addition, a comparative analysis of the differences between the US and German legal implementations on GAFA from the perspective of behavioral economics (Frank 2020) is conducted. More directly targeted on the transactional side of data, studies have focused on online display advertising in the advertising ecosystem (Geradin and Katsifis 2019). It has been pointed out that hidden data practices, which may be employed as a means to maintain substantial market dominance instead of improvement of efficiency, may pose a serious concern for competition authorities from a privacy perspective (Kemp 2020). In addition, Fuchikawa (2020), who discusses the use of unfair trade practices in Japanese Antimonoply Act, has a significant connection with this chapter. He points out that it would be desirable to simplify the evaluation of market definition and the burden of proof, especially in the case of private litigation. Hayashi and Arai (2019) discuss the issues to be considered when enforcing competition policy, such as how to define the market, how to measure market dominance, and how to apply abuse of dominant position. It should be referred to as a basic discussion on competition law enforcement for digital platforms.

On the other hand, these studies do not discuss the need for confidence building in the market and its legal and economic underpinnings, which are the main focus of this chapter. In this context, we focus on competition law issues involving data transaction, and attempt to bridge the gap between the effectiveness of law enforcement and the legal theories that support the maintenance of competition in the marketplace.

This chapter has been structured as follows. In Sect. 2, we discuss the legal issues and explain the economics of the applicability of competition law to DPFs. Section 3 discusses issues regarding the Consumer Superiority Guidelines in terms of consideration and impediment to fair competition.[4] Section 4 critically addresses the Digital Platform Transparency Act legally and economically. Section 5 discusses the possible scope for an amendment to labeling regulations. Section 6 is the conclusion.

Here is an example of provisions pertaining to data fiduciary, which serves as a reference for the following discussion.

NY State Privacy Bill: Clarification of Data Fiduciary Provisions

In the bill, data fiduciary is defined as follows. (Article 1102)

Data Fiduciary Provisions (Summary)

Privacy Risk

"Privacy risks" are defined as "potentially adverse consequences for consumers arising from the processing of personal data" and examples include (but are not limited to) the following

1. Direct/indirect financial loss or economic damage
2. Physical damage

[4] See the JFTC's website: https://www.jftc.go.jp/en/legislation_gls/imonopoly_guidelines_files/191217DPconsumerGL.pdf.

3. Mental damage
4. Substantial inconvenience or waste of time
5. Adverse consequences or decisions in employment, credit, insurance, housing, education, personal certification, health care and related services
6. Damage to reputation and trust
7. Commercial communication (e.g., advertising) not desired by the consumer
8. Price discrimination
9. Potential adverse effects on individuals that are not reasonably foreseeable to consumers but foreseeable to administrators
10. Other adverse consequences/impacts on the private life of the individual.

However, this does not grant the DPF any comprehensive obligation of care for consumers.

NY State Privacy Bill: Clarification of "Consumer's Rights"

In response to a request from a consumer, a data controller shall disclose how it processes personal information. At the request of the consumer, the data controller must disclose to the consumer how it processes personal data and (if so) the names of the third parties to whom it has passed such information. In addition, the data controller must provide the consumer with a copy of the personal data being processed free of charge up to twice a year.

Upon request from the consumer, the data controller must correct any inaccurate information about the consumer without undue delay. 3.

In response to a request from a consumer, a data controller must erase, without undue delay, any information relating to the consumer. (*The following three items are further detailed: 1. conditions for erasure; 2. what to do if the data controller is obliged to erase information that has been disclosed to a third party; 3. exceptions if the consumer's rights in this section are not recognized)

4. [Termination of processing] If requested by the consumer (*there are four categories mentioned as types of requests), the controller must terminate the processing of personal information.

⇒The key point is that all of these are stated as "consumer rights"

5. Upon request from the consumer, the data controller provides the personal data provided by the consumer to the controller in machine-readable form.

⇒Data portability is an ongoing issue in Japan. However, there is a concern that simply granting data portability rights will only strengthen the oligopoly of DPF operators, as in the case of the DTP (Data Transfer Project) that was undertaken collaboratively by Google, Facebook, and others.

6. [Profiling] Consumers should not be governed by decisions based solely on legal or similarly significant profiling.

7. The controller must inform the third party to whom the personal data has been provided of any correction, erasure or processing of personal data carried out in

accordance with 2, 3 and 4 above. The controller must inform the consumer of the existence of such a third party if the consumer so requests.

8. [Disclosure] The controller shall disclose without delay information regarding actions taken in response to requests under 1–5.

2 Applicability of Competition Law

First, with respect to the applicabilion of the Antimonopoly Act and the Act against Unjustifiable Premiums and Misleading Representations, Article 2, Paragraph 9, Item 5 of the Antimonopoly Act has a unique regulation on the abuse of a superior bargaining position regulation, providing as follows. A person who, taking advantage of the superiority of his or her business position over the counterparty, acts unfairly in light of normal business practices and falls under any of the following (a) Inducing the counterparty with whom the counterparty continuously conducts transactions to purchase goods or services other than those pertaining to the transactions (b) Causing the counterparty with whom the counterparty continuously conducts transactions to provide money, services, or other economic benefits for the counterparty's own use (c) Refusing to receive goods pertaining to a transaction from the counterparty of the transaction, having the counterparty of the transaction take back the goods after receiving them from the counterparty of the transaction, delaying payment of the consideration for the transaction to the counterparty of the transaction or reducing the amount thereof, or otherwise setting or changing the terms of the transaction to the disadvantage of the counterparty of the transaction, or conducting the transaction or change the terms of the transaction, or conduct the transaction to the disadvantage of the counterparty.[5] Based on this provision, the JFTC has issued guidelines for DPF in terms of the consumer transaction, which is titled "Guidelines Concerning Abuse of a Superior Bargaining Position in Transactions between Digital Platform Operators and Consumers that Provide Personal Information, etc." (hereinafter "Consumer Superiority Guidelines").

If the DPF operator's acquisition or use of personal information in an unfair manner causes consumers disadvantage and adverse effects on fair and free competition, issues may arise under the Japanese Antimonopoly Act. The Consumer Superiority Guidelines describe what kind of conduct related to the acquisition of personal information or use of acquired personal information on a DPF may constitute abuse of a superior bargaining position in view of promoting the transparency of the Antimonopoly Act enforcement and improvement of predictability for DPF operators.

Basic concepts of the regulation on abuse of a superior bargaining position in the context of the Consumer Superiority Guidelines are as follows;

---

[5] See the JFTC's website: https://www.jftc.go.jp/en/legislation_gls/amended_ama09/20122501.pdf.

The trade terms are basically left to the independent judgement of the trading parties. However, in transactions between enterprises and consumers, there exists disparity in the quality and quantity of information and negotiating power between consumers and enterprises, and the trade terms are likely to be unilaterally unfair to consumers. If a DPF operator with a superior bargaining position over consumers who are the counterparties to transactions unjustifiably causes, in light of normal business practices, disadvantage to consumers by taking advantage of such position, the DPF operator not only may affect the free and independent judgements of consumers, but also is likely to gain competitive advantage over its competitors. Because such conduct is likely to impede fair competition, it is prohibited under the Antimonopoly Act as abuse of a superior bargaining position, a type of unfair trade practices.

The asymmetry in the value of data between DPF operators and consumers allows the former to covertly exploit consumers using personal information, etc. (e.g., targeting prices to vulnerable consumers with few external options, differentiation of services and opportunities). (i.e., price (targeting price), service, and opportunity differentiation). For example, there is a potential problem regarding the common point service (unilateral disadvantageous change of terms and conditions, etc.). The JFTC report "Investigation into the actual status of transactions related to the common point service" (June 12, 2020) indicates how personal information may be misused to the detriment of competition.

Although different from the framework of competition restriction and competition exclusion in the ordinary competition law, the Consumer Superiority Guidelines are intended to regulate the behavior of those who engage in competition and to fully exercise the function of competition in order to achieve the optimal allocation in the market. They mainly prohibit the exploitation of the value of data in order to prevent the moral hazard of DPFs. Also, they are intended to prohibit exploiting consumers as well as conducting price targeting (i.e., to prevent the development of a market where quality is not guaranteed) in order to avoid adverse selection.

3 Issues Relating to the Consumer Superiority Guidelines

3.1 Whether the Exchange of Data Between DPF Operators and Consumers Constitutes a "Transaction"?

With respect to DPF services, most consumers generally perceive that they use DPF services free of charge, rather than that they pay for the DPF services with their own personal information. In this regard, whether the consumers' personal information is provided to the DPF operators in consideration of their services, which is a problem identified in the Consumer Superiority Guidelines, does not seem to be a critical issue here. By contrast, in the Directive (EU) 2019/770 on contracts for the supply of digital content and services, the requirement of 'data as counter-performance' was not introduced into the language of the directive. From a competition law perspective, the crucial issues are, regardless of the presence or degree of "data as counter-performance", whether consumers are in a position to be exploited by DPF operators, and whether the consumers are compelled, as a condition of the provision of DPF services, to provide their personal data.

3.2 Impediment to Fair Competition by Abuse of a Superior Bargaining Position in Transactions with Consumers

Abuse of a superior bargaining position is regarded as "infringement of the foundation of free competition" in the context of the Antimonopoly Act. However, the JFTC's enforcement of the Antimonopoly Act has been focused on transactions between "businesses". The prevailing construction of "the impediment to fair competition", which is the legal term representing the anticompetitive effect of abuse of a superior bargaining position, is the anticompetitive harm resulting from (a) competition between the abusing business and its competitors (third parties), or (b) competition between the abused business and its competitors (third parties) (so-called indirect competition infringement theory). However, if we consider the abuse of a superior bargaining position in the context of the relationship between a DPF operator and its users, at least in the previous situation (b), the abused party is not a business operator but instead the "consumers" and theoretically there is no competitive relationship among individual consumers. It is thus difficult to explicitly explain the Consumer Superiority Guidelines with the theory of indirect competition infringement.

The issue of asymmetry in the value of data between DPF operators and consumers, which allows companies to secretly exploit consumers with their personal information (i.e., to differentiate prices, services, and opportunities by targeting vulnerable consumers with few external options) is also difficult to be tackled based on the theory of indirect competition infringement. The possibility of exploitation, namely price, service, and opportunity differentiation targeting vulnerable consumers with few external options, may rise because consumers may not be aware of the value of their data.

3.3 Position of Economics on Issues Such as Consideration and Impediment to Fair Competition

Economics does not consider consideration only in terms of money. Whether the terms and conditions of a DPF service constitute exploitation or not is subjective unless there is an objective standard. Without the standard, the predictability problem may arise, and it would be difficult to adopt a policy.

In this context, the standard of exploitation is considered to be the act of using market dominance in a market (transaction) to allocate resources non-competitively, thereby diverting the incentives of consumers and hindering the development of the market in the medium to long term.

It should be however noted that the abuse of a superior bargaining position in consumer transactions is difficult to verify because the causal relationships between the abuse of a superior bargaining position and the impediment to fair competition related to third parties, and the impact on competition of the business subject to the abuse are not clear from an economic perspective.

4 Specific Digital Platform Transparency Act and Its Limitations

The basic philosophy of the Digital Platform Transparency Act (hereinafter in this section referred to as "Act") could be as follows. DPFs contribute to an increase in benefits for users. They play an important role in increasing the vitality of and realizing the sustainable development of the Japanese economy and society. In light of this, measures for improving transparency and fairness of transactions conducted on DPFs should be implemented, primarily based on voluntary and proactive initiatives by DPF operators, with government involvement or other regulations kept to the minimum. DPF operators can adequately exercise their originality and ingenuity, and mutual understanding in business relationship between DPF operators and product providers is facilitated.

The main measures to be taken under the Act are as follows:

The first is measures targeting specified DPF operators. According to the Act, the authority concerned will designate DPF businesses whose transparency and fairness in trading should be improved as "specified digital platform providers" with a cabinet order. The specified providers, whether domestic or overseas, are subject to the following rules.[6]

1. Requiring specified DPF operators to disclose their business information, e.g., terms and conditions of trading. The Act is to require specified DPF operators to disclose terms and conditions and give prior notices of any change thereof to the DPF users.
2. Requesting specified DPF operators to develop procedures and systems in a voluntary manner. The Act is to request such providers to develop procedures and systems in accordance with the guidelines specified by the Minister of Economy, Trade and Industry (METI).
3. Requiring specified DPF operators to submit a report on the results of self-assessment and requiring the METI Minister to assess the report. The Act is to require such providers to submit a report, every fiscal year, on their current situations of items [1] and [2] above with the results of self-assessment on such

[6] The categories and sizes of businesses are to be stipulated under cabinet order.

situations to the METI Minister, and then the Minister to assess the situations of business operation based on the report and publicize the assessment results.

The Act also requires METI to establish a system in which METI should request the JFTC to exercise certain measures under the Antimonopoly Act if METI finds any cases which are suspected of violating the Antimonopoly Act.

Similar to the EU P2B regulations,[7] the Act is not directly aimed at consumer protection. It encourages fair competition among DPFs from the perspective of protecting the interests of users of products, etc. On the other hand, this does not negate the purpose of reflexively protecting consumers, which is the purpose (Article 1) of the Act, stating "protection of the interests of users 'etc.' of products, etc.").

In this regard, Article 5, Paragraph 2, Item 2 of the Act stipulates the obligation of specified DPF operators to disclose to general users (i.e., consumers) specific matters (such as information on the order in which search results are displayed, conditions regarding the acquisition and use of purchase data, and other matters designated by the Ministerial Ordinance). This provision is aimed to ensure that users of the provision of goods, etc. are treated fairly on the DPF. For example, when consumers search for products on a DPF, they tend to choose the product displayed at the top of the search result page. If the search algorithm adopted by the DPF is unfair, it will distort the consumer's choice and in turn impede fair competition among sellers (providers of goods, etc.). In other words, making it possible for consumers to understand what factors are used to display search results has the effect of keeping "sellers" competition fair. This is why the Act, which protects the interests of sellers, requires "disclosure of the main factors of the search to consumers" (Article 5, Paragraph 2, Item 2 (a)).

The Act is a step forward in terms of stipulating disclosure obligations and measures to be taken by specified DPF operators. However, it also has limitations in that the scope of regulation is limited to the online shopping mall and the app store market. Search services and social networking services are excluded. The Act aims to protect the interests of users of products by imposing disclosure obligations on DPFs and placing a corresponding burden on influential businesses for the development of a free and fair market. Accordingly, it is necessary to limit and clarify the scope of influential business operators. In addition, Article 13 of the Act stipulates that the METI may request the JFTC to take action against a specified DPF operator if the Minister finds that the conduct of the DPF operator violates Article 19 (Unfair Trade Practices) of the Antimonopoly Act. However, the fact that the METI has the authority to determine whether or not a violation of the Antimonopoly Act occurs may make the provision ineffective. The legal requirements of unfair trade practices, including the harm requirement "a likelihood of impediment to fair competition", are extremely technical and abstract. We are concerned about whether the METI, rather than the JFTC, which is the specialized and exclusive enforcement agency of the Antimonopoly Act, can make a judgment on such highly normative requirements. This may be a way to broaden the range of competition policy by increasing the

[7] Regulation (EU) 2019/1150 of the European Parliament and of the Council of 20 June 2019 on promoting fairness and transparency for business users of online intermediation services.

Table 1 Prisoner's dilemma situation

	Consumers	
	Short term behavior	Long term behavior
DPF operator's short-term behavior	($\alpha 1$, $\beta 1$)	($\alpha 2$, $\beta 2$)
Long-term behavior	($\alpha 3$, $\beta 3$)	($\alpha 4$, $\beta 4$)

The contents of the parentheses are (DPF operator's payoff, consumer's payoff)
$\alpha 3 < \alpha 1 < \alpha 4 < \alpha 2$, $\beta 2 < \beta 1 < \beta 3 < \beta 4$

number of regulators in charge of competition policy, but the concern also arises as to whether a unified and uniform competition policy can be maintained from an enforcement perspective.

On the other hand, we provide a critique of the Act also from an economics standpoint. The part that merely requires the disclosure of information to general users (consumers) in order to ensure that users who provide products, etc. are treated fairly on the DPF is considered to be a far-fetched discipline from an economic perspective.

This is unlikely to provide appropriate incentives for those who act in a Nash equilibrium manner, seeking only short-term profits in a prisoner's dilemma situation (Table 1).

The Nash equilibrium is (short-term behavior for DPF operators, short-term behavior for consumers). Here, what is essentially needed is to transform the magnitude of the gains of $\alpha 1$ and $\alpha 3$ so that the firms adopt long-term behavior and achieve the equilibrium of (long-term behavior, long-term behavior).Therefore, the argument here is the need for regulations that increase the cost of choosing the $\alpha 1$ behavior.

5 The Importance of the Act Against Unjustifiable Premiums and Misleading Representations

Articles 2(4) and 2(5) of the Act on Unjustifiable Premiums and Misleading Representations (hereinafter referred to as "Anti-Misleading Advertisement Act") only regulate representations made by a "business operator" with respect to the goods or services it provides. In view of the fact that the Anti-Misleading Advertisement Act is the main regulation of customer attraction, is this requirement appropriate when considering the regulation of customer attraction in the digital age? For example, stealth marketing and affiliate advertising may fall outside the scope of the Anti-Misleading Advertisement Act owing to this requirement.

Basically, when a DPF operator operates a DPF marketplace, the actual seller of products (i.e., the supply entity) is not the DPF operator in question, but the business operator who exhibits products on the DPF. The DPF operator is an intermediary for the sale (seller) and purchase (consumers). Therefore, if the seller is an exhibitor and makes misleading representations, it should be primarily responsible for the misleading representations.

However, the DPF operator should not be exempted from responsibility for the misleading representations only by asserting that it is an "intermediary". The issue of who is responsible must not, in principle, affect the efficiency of society (social welfare) as a whole (as long as the DPF operator is allowed to seek reimbursement from the responsible entity). Considering the transaction costs, it is reasonable to make the DPF operator liable (jointly and severally in some cases) to a certain extent.

A mislabeling case of Matsuzaka Beef (Cease-and-Desist Order against Keio Department Store and Meidi-ya Sangyo (2002 (Hai) No. 27 (October 25, 2002, JFTC)) is worthy of reference. Although the Keio Department Store was not directly involved in Meidi-ya's deceptive practices, the meat was improperly labeled at the meat department in the name of Meidi-ya. It is believed that the mislabeling was based on the fact that Keio Department Store was in a position to give instructions and advice to Meidi-ya Sangyo regarding the operation of the meat sales floor, but did not take sufficient measures to check and prevent the mislabeling, thereby causing misunderstanding among consumers. (Takagi et al., Fair Trade No. 633, p. 67 (2003)).

Economic support for this argument is as follows: What is important here is whether DPF operators will change their own behavior from short-term to long-term behavior if they are obliged to bear the risk of incapacity and monitoring costs. Nevertheless, making DPF operators also bear the risk and costs within a certain range (jointly and severally) can be a necessary condition for behavioral change, but hardly a sufficient condition. Put differently, the DPF operators' fulfillment of the obligation requires to be monitored, but proper monitoring may not be done.

Therefore, in order to achieve behavioral change, it will be necessary to analyze the incentive structure for businesses and take appropriate measures. The future task is to consider the check evaluation of businesses that are conducting proper monitoring and the public procurement system based on the check evaluation.

Reference: Case of Amazon Japan requesting revocation of a cease-and-desist order (part of the judgment)

- The term "business operator that has made an unfair labeling that falls under Article 5, item 2 of the Anti-Misleading Advertisement Act" means a business operator who has been involved in the content of the labeling, and the term "business operator that has been involved in the content of the labeling" means not only a business operator who has actively determined the content of the labeling by itself or jointly with others, but also a business operator who has received an explanation from another business operator regarding the content of the labeling determined or to be determined. It is reasonable to conclude that the term "business operator" includes not only those who have actively determined the contents of labeling by themselves or jointly with others, but also those who have received explanations from other business firms about the contents of labeling determined or to be determined by other business firms and have agreed to use such labeling as their own labeling, and those who have entrusted other business firms to determine the contents of labeling even though they are able to determine the contents of labeling by themselves.

- Considering the fact that X was the seller of the five products in question, and that this fact was also indicated on the respective product pages, it is reasonable to conclude that X constructed the display on the website in advance so that the double price display would be displayed in certain cases, and that the double price display of the products was actually displayed in accordance with this mechanism. In consideration of the fact that X constructed the display on the website in advance so that the double price display would occur in certain cases, and that X represented itself as the seller of the five products and sold the five products in accordance with the said mechanism, X can be said to be a business operator who was involved in determining the content of the display of the five products.
- In addition, it is X who decides whether or not to display the reference prices entered by the suppliers or sellers on the Website, and it is X who selects one of those reference prices to be displayed on the website based on the results of the system's selection based on some criteria. As a result, it is recognized that the reference price entered by the supplier or the seller was displayed for each of the displays in question, and therefore, X should be said to have been involved in the content of the display of each of the displays in question.

Reference: Chujitsuya Case (Supreme Court, November 30, 1995, Minshu, Vol. 49, No. 9, p. 2972)

- In this case, the tenant store had such an appearance that ordinary shoppers could not help but mistakenly believe that the pet store was run by Chujitsuya. And, since Chujitsuya created or was involved in the creation of the right appearance by, for example, displaying the trademark of Chujitsuya on the outside of the store in question and concluding a contract with [the tenant] for the opening of a new store and the use of the store with the same content, Chujitsuya is liable for the violation by analogy with Article 23 of the Commercial Code (Article 9 of the current Companies Act) for transactions between the shopper and the tenant store.

  ⇒This appearance of right doctrine may be helpful in the interpretation of the Anti-Misleading Advertisement Act.

Reference: Yahoo Auction case (Nagoya District Court, March 28, 2008, Hanrei Jihou No. 2029, p. 89)

- "There is no sufficient evidence to find that the defendant actively intervened in transactions between users and made efforts to conclude such transactions, and it cannot be said that the contract in question has the nature of an intermediary.…As a matter of principle in this User Agreement, the defendant is obligated to construct a defect-free system and provide this service to the users, including the plaintiffs." The specific contents of the obligation are determined by comprehensively considering the social conditions surrounding Internet auctions at the time of the provision of the service, relevant laws and regulations, the technical level of the system, the costs required for the construction and maintenance of the system, the effects of the introduction of the system, and the convenience of the system users.

⇒According to the prevalent interpretation in Japan, DPFs are deemed to be mere "place" providers and thus have no responsibility for the customer's loss. This interpretation is however not in line with the actual business operation and market conditions. Even in the case where DPFs are not directly involved in the transaction between the seller and buyer, they contribute to the conclusion of the sales contract. Also, in some past cases, DPF business operators were even observed not fulfilling the duty of care. Thus, whether a DPF is responsible or not should be judged on a case-by-case basis.

6 Conclusion

DPF operators should be subject to the duty of "information fiduciary" (duty of care, duty of loyalty, and duty of confidentiality) as a general guiding principle (preferably by legislative allowance). The Digital Platform Transparency Act is not an end point of consumer protection in dealings with DPF, but only a milestone. The legal formality of being an "intermediary" alone should not prevent DPF operators from being found liable. In principle, the question of who is responsible must not affect the efficiency of society (social welfare) as a whole. It is thus not appropriate to unilaterally place the burden of seller's incapacity on consumers, considering the enforcement costs of consumers and the risk of the primarily responsible party's inability to meet the obligations. From an economic point of view, it is not appropriate to make consumers bear such risks unilaterally.

From an economic point of view, new DPF businesses are basically free of any regulation. The new business is used to promote IT and is an engine of economic growth. The obligations to be imposed on DPF operators are the necessary conditions for the market to grow more. And the fact that freedom of business activity is ensured gives customers a sense of security, which represents a chance for DPF operators to develop into a larger business.

On the other hand, the legal form of intermediation and the burden of risk should not be discussed only in specific countries. International cooperation and collaborative efforts are especially necessary for the increasingly globalized digital market. Furthermore, it is necessary to consider evidence-based regulations. It should be noted that there are different levels of evidence.

Given the fact that it is difficult to promote discipline and business development based on randomized controlled trials, the future challenge is to respond based on empirical verification using various methods of measurement. In this sense, research suggests that, on average, no single platform provides substantially greater consumer surplus than the sum of two competing platforms. This average result at the market level is due to the differential effects between the users of the two platforms' integration. In particular, the results show that users of the acquiring platform benefit from the merger, while users of the acquired platform exit the market. Some of these exits may be driven by the importance of repeat transactions, reduced product diversity, and switching costs. These results do not take into account the possibility that some deconfliction may have occurred due to mergers. In that case, measuring activity using platform data would underestimate the true amount of surplus created in the market (Farronato et al. 2020).

The contribution of this chapter to the advencement of competition law is that it organizes the discipline of competition law on DPF as a necessity from the aspect of ensuring trust, and that it discusses the applicability of labeling regulations. In this way, the scope of consumer protection for DPFs is supplemented by competition law, and the possibility of realizing more appropriate competition in the market is shown, which has not been seen in previous discussions of competition law and is considered to be original. A limitation of this chapter is that it is based on the system of Japanese law. However, the subject of this chapter is the applicability of competition law and labeling regulations to the conduct of DPF, and it is applicable to the discussion of not only Japanese law but also competition laws around the world.

7 Summary

In the digital market, giant platform (PF) providers, represented by global players such as GAFA, are expanding their market position through the use of big data obtained from consumers. Since digital platform (DPF) firms are characterized by their tendency to monopolize by oligopolize the market, there has been an increasing number of competition law violations by DPF operators, the development of various legal systems, and academic discussions with the aim of protecting consumer rights and ensuring transparency and fairness in the trading environment. DPF operators should be subject to the duty of "information fiduciary" (duty of care, duty of loyalty, and duty of confidentiality) as a general guiding principle (preferably by legislative allowance). The Digital Platform Transparency Act is not an end point of consumer protection in dealings with DPF, but only a milestone. The legal formality of being an "intermediary" alone should not prevent DPF operators from being found liable. In principle, the question of who is responsible must not affect the efficiency of society (social welfare) as a whole. It is thus not appropriate to unilaterally place the risk of seller's incapacity on consumers, considering the enforcement costs of consumers and the risk of the primarily responsible party's inability to meet the obligations. From an economic point of view, it is not appropriate to make consumers bear such risks unilaterally. The contribution of this chapter to the development of competition law is that it organizes the discipline of competition law on DPF as a necessity from the aspect of ensuring trust and discusses the applicability of labeling regulations. In this way, the scope of consumer protection for DPFs is supplemented by competition law, and the possibility of realizing more appropriate competition in the market is shown, which has not been seen in previous discussions of competition law and is considered to be original. A limitation of this chapter is that it is based on the system of Japanese law. However, the subject of this chapter is the applicability of competition law and labeling regulations to the conduct of DPF, and it is applicable to the discussion of not only Japanese competition law but also competition laws around the world.

References

Farronato C, Fong J, Fradkin A (2020) Dog eat dog: measuring network effects using a digital platform merger. NBER working paper 28047

Frank L (2020) Boundedly rational users and the fable of break-ups: why breaking-up big tech companies probably will not promote competition from behavioural economics perspective. World Competition 43(3):373–384

Fuchikawa K (2020) Regulations of digital platform markets under the Japanese antimonopoly act: does the regulation of unfair trade practices solve the Gordian knot of digital markets? Antitrust Bull 65(1):102–119

Geradin D, Katsifis D (2019) An EU competition law analysis of online display advertising in the programmatic age. 55–96. Received 22 Jan 2019, Accepted 23 Jan 2019

Hayashi S, Arai K (2019) How competition law should react in the age of big data and artificial intelligence. Antitrust Bull 64(3):447–456

Jedlicková B (2019) Digital polyopoly. World Competition 42(3):309–333

Kemp K (2020) Concealed data practices and competition law: why privacy matters. 628–672. Received 15 Oct 2020, Accepted 16 Oct 2020

Loderer GT, Picht PG (2019) Framing algorithms: competition law and (other) regulatory tools. World Competition 42(3):391–417

Takagi M, Nakayama T, Yako Y (2003) Mislabeling cases concerning meat ((1) cease and desist order against Hayashiken Sangyo Co., (2) cease and desist order against Keio Department Store and Meidi-ya Sangyo). Fair Trade 633(7):67–71

Chapter 10
Recent Issues Concerning Licensing of Standard Essential Patents

1 Introduction

In recent years, disputes over licensing of Standard Essential Patents (SEPs) have arisen in many countries around the world due to the proliferation of standards and the increasing complexity of the technologies required for such standards. In future, SEPs licensing transactions between different industries are expected to increase, especially in the fields of manufacturing, such as automobiles and construction machinery.

For example, in the field of wireless communications, Avanci, a patent pool management company that licenses its SEPs for the Internet of Things (IoT) field, such as connected cars and smart meters, has concluded SEP licensing agreements with a number of automobile manufacturers regarding the mobile communication standard. Avanci is engaged in lawsuits with some automakers over SEP licenses. For example, in Germany, the Mannheim District Court granted an injunction against Daimler, a German automobile manufacturer, in the Nokia v. Daimler case. The injunction restrained Daimler from selling approximately half of its automobiles in Germany. If this ruling became final, Daimler's annual loss reportedly would have been as much as 4.5 billion euros (approximately 560 billion yen). The background to such lawsuits is the scheme in which SEP holders choose to collect patent license fees from end-product manufacturers (e.g., Daimler) instead of upstream standard implementers (component suppliers). This is because SEP holders expect higher license fees by targeting end-product manufacturers to enforce their rights without licensing their SEPs to upstream component suppliers. The manufacturing industry is however concerned that if this scheme is rolled out, end-product manufacturers and component manufacturers in the supply chain will face high licensing costs

The original version of this chapter was revised in the Reference section. A correction to the chapter can be found at
https://doi.org/10.1007/978-981-99-5310-3_12

S. Hayashi and K. Arai, *Digitalization and Competition Policy in Japan*,
https://doi.org/10.1007/978-981-99-5310-3_10

while receiving insufficient compensation, which making their businesses unviable. In other words, this is the problem of bearing the cost of patent licensing fees in the supply chain. This is also related to issues under the Antimonopoly Act, e.g., unfair restraint of trade, and abuse of a superior bargaining position. In fact, at a meeting held by the Conceptual Framework Committee, Intellectual Property Strategy Headquarter at the Cabinet Office in Japan, particpants from the business community have suggested that certain guidelines should be established on how the burden should be allocated within the supply chain.

In addition, amid the wide inconsistency between claims of SEP holders and those of potential licensees with respect to the licensing terms of SEPs, attention is being paid to the licensing negotiation process. For example, in the German case of Philips v. Wiko, the Higher District Court of Karlsruhe held that the license terms offered by the SEP holder must explain not only the amount of the patent license fee and its calculation method, but also why they are non-discriminatory and non-exploitative. Further, in the case that the SEP holder has licensed its SEPs to third parties in the past, (i) if the SEP holder has granted licenses to all licensees under the same terms and conditions, then the license agreement at issue should be concluded under those terms and conditions; (ii) if the SEP holder has granted licenses under different terms and conditions to different licensees, then the SEP holder should at least explain to the other party to the negotiations to what extent and on what substantive grounds such other party is treated differently from the other previous licensees with respect to the principal license terms provided in the license agreement at issue. Moreover, the treatment of claim charts in notices of infringement is also controversial. Thus, from the viewpoint of the process of resolving disputes between the parties, the need for discipline and rules on the provision of necessary information between the parties has become an important issue. This is partly because, with inter-industry disputes taking center stage in SEP licensing disputes, major players in Japanese industry, including the automobile industry, are exposed to the risk of SEP injunctions or other actions. This is also the reason the Japanese Patent Office (JPO) stated in an official report, titled "Interim Summary of the Patent System Appropriate for the Era of AI-IoT Technology", that the direction of injunction and negotiations between different industries will be further examined in the review of the Japanese patent system.

Patent pools are also controversial. A patent pool refers to a consortium in which multiple persons who have rights to a certain technology concentrate their respective patents or their rights to license patents to a corporate or organizational entity. Members of the patent pool also obtain the patent licenses necessary for their business operations from the corporate or organizational entity. Patent pools generally bring benefits to both right holders and implementers in terms of (i) reduction of contract negotiation costs (one-stop licensing), (ii) avoidance of disputes, and (iii) reduction of the so-called "tragedy of the anticommons." However, patent pools are not a panacea. In fact, there are some cases where the licensing fees offered by patent pools are still high. For example, in the case of the aforementioned Avanci, there are influential patent holders (the so-called outsiders) which do not join Avanci. Besides, the need to deal with excessive royalties demanded by Avanci under competition law has been repeatedly expressed. It also seems that patent pools should be analyzed separately from joint licensing organizations. While one-stop licensing organizations can streamline negotiations, there are concerns that excessive license fees may be unilaterally set and imposed on implementors. Currently, the Japanese government is studying how to ensure transparency in the royalty-setting process.

In light of the above, this chapter discusses (1) how the burden of SEP compensation should be allocated within the supply chain, (2) the evaluation of patent pool, and (3) the need to establish rules of the provision of information among parties during the negotiation process, given the wide gap in claims among parties regarding the licensee and license conditions.

In the following Sect. 2, we will discuss some of the issues related to the recent patent cases in Europe. In Sect. 3, we will discuss some of the issues specified in Sect. 1.

The reason for focusing on Europe is that, as described below, there is a wealth of case studies available on the issues discussed in this chapter, and that the policy positions of Europe and Japan have a lot in common. For example, in November 2020, the European Commission adopted an Action Plan titled "Making the most of the EU's innovative potential—An intellectual property action plan to support the EU's recovery and resilience" (COM/2020/760), which aims to improve the transparency and predictability of SEP licenses. In the short term, the Commission will promote industry-led initiatives to reduce friction and litigation between players in certain sectors, and to achieve its goals for SEP licensing, taking into account increased legal certainty and reduced litigation costs. These aims have much in common with those of Japan. For these reasons, this chapter will refer primarily to the discussions in Europe.

2 Development of European Court Cases

2.1 Huawei V. ZTE (C-170/13) Preliminary Judgment of the Court of Justice of the European Union (CJEU): A Starting Point

This decision set the course for subsequent judicial decisions in that it provided a framework for license negotiations based on the duty of good faith negotiation between the parties, which serves as a criterion for determining whether a request for an injunction based on a SEP violates Article 102 of the Treaty on the Operation of the European Union (TFEU) or not.

In this decision, the CJEU held that the SEP holder does not abuse its dominant position within the meaning of Article 102 TFEU, if (1) the SEP holder, prior to filing a lawsuit, warns the alleged infringer by designating the SEP being infringed and specifying the manner of infringement, and in response, the alleged infringer expresses its willingness to enter into a FRAND license agreement; (2) the SEP holder presents to the infringer a specific, written offer for a license on FRAND terms, specifying the royalty and the way in which it is to be calculated; and (3) the alleged infringer continues to use the SEP without responding in good faith to the offer of the SEP holder in accordance with widely accepted commercial practices in the field in question.

Since this decision, litigation concerning SEPs in Europe has been debating over the consideration of specific requirements regarding the duty of good faith negotiation, referring to the criteria set forth in this decision.

2.2 Recent Court Decisions in Germany

Since 2020, court cases, including the German cases of Sisvel v. Haier, Nokia v. Daimler, and Sharp v. Daimler, and the British cases of Unwired Planet v. Huawei and Conversant v. Huawei/ZTE. have been appearing at a furious pace.

In Sisvel v. Haier, Sisvel, a NPE that holds SEPs related to GSM standards transferred from Nokia, sought an injunction and damages against Haier, an electronics manufacturer, on the grounds of SEP infringement. Haier rejected Sisvel's initial license offer, and although Haier expressed its willingness to accept the license by presenting a counter-offer, Sisvel rejected it. The parties exchanged mutual proposals, but in the end, no agreement was reached. Sisvel then filed for an injunction against Haier in Düsseldorf District Court, which, for the first time since the CJEU preliminary ruling in Huawei v. ZTE, ruled in favor of the SEP holder's request for an injunction. Nevertheless, the Düsseldorf Higher Regional Court reversed the district court's decision, upholding Haier's FRAND defense. Sisvel then appealed to the Federal Court of Justice (BGH), the highest court in Germany, and the BGH reversed the High Court decision and allowed the SEP holder to exercise its rights.

The BGH's decision focused on the prevention of holdouts. Holdout refers to the situation where, in view of the possible bad faith response from the implementer, the right holder may hesitate to join standard setting organization (SSO), or have difficutly in recouping the costs spent on research and development to obtain a SEP. Generally, if a SEP holder makes a FRAND commitment, it is required to license under FRAND terms. Accordingly, if the court finds that the SEP holder's offer does not meet the FRAND requirement, the SEP holder will not be allowed to exercise its rights. Therefore, an implementer expecting that the exercise of SEP rights is not likely to be allowed may take advantage of the situation and not respond to license negotiations in good faith.

Specifically, the BGH strictly interpreted the criteria for "willingness to take a patent license" to mean the following situation. (1) The SEP holder is not required either to inform the implementer of the fact of infringement by showing a claim chart, or to provide a detailed technical explanation; intead, notifying the fact of infringement and identifying the infringed patent would be sufficient. (2) The implementer must consult an outside expert if it is unable to confirm infringement on its own. (3) As long as the license is on FRAND terms, the implementer must express its intention to accept the FRAND license unconditionally, and it must negotiate in good faith with the SEP holder and must not unreasonably delay the license negotiation. Furthermore, the non-discriminatory requirement in the FRAND conditions should be interpreted in light of the actual circumstances of the transaction, and it does not require the SEP holder to offer the implementer the same contents and conditions as the most favorable past license conditions, since the FRAND conditions may naturally differ depending on the individual transaction situation.

Next, in Nokia v. Daimler, Nokia filed a lawsuit against Daimler in the Mannheim, Deutscheldorf, and Munich District Courts at the same time, alleging that Daimler's embedded telematics control unit (TCU) infringed Nokia's SEP. The issue in this case was whether the "licence to all" concept, which states that the SEP holder must license to all entities that wish to obtain a license, regardless of their stages of the transaction in the supply chain (Tier 1 or Tier 2), constitutes a FRAND obligation. Daimler, as the implementer of Nokia's SEP, argued that it was a FRAND obligation of the SEP holder. The Mannheim District Court found that Daimler responded to Nokia's infringement notice by stating that Nokia should negotiate with Daimler's component supplier and that the calculation basis of the royalties should be the Smallest Saleable Patent Practicing Unit (SSPPU), without negotiating with Nokia for about two years. The court thus denied Daimler's claim, holding that Daimler had no intention to accept the license. It should be however noted that the Mannheim District Court did not squarely address the question of whether the concept of "license to all" is the FRAND obligation of the SEP holder. Yet, according to the news report at the time of writing (June 2021), Nokia and Daimler concluded a license agreement for Nokia's SEP (details of the agreement are not disclosed).

Daimler reportedly paid undisclosed royalties to Nokia, and Nokia withdrawed its lawsuit against Daimler, and Daimler withdrawed its antitrust complaint at the European Commission.

In the Sharp v. Daimler case, Sharp filed a lawsuit in the Munich District Court alleging that Daimler's vehicles equipped with LTE wireless technology infringed Sharp's SEP. The district court found that Daimler infringed Sharp's SEP, and rejected Daimler's defense that Sharp's exercise of its rights was in violation of the FRAND commitment. The court also rejected Daimler's argument that Nokia should license the component suppliers based on the "license to all" concept, and ruled that an implementer must make a declaration of intent to unconditionally receive a FRAND license as long as the terms and conditions of the license FRAND.

The court held that Daimler had no intention to accept the license in the first place, and granted Sharp's request for an injunction. Sharp and Daimler eventually settled the case and entered into an LTE patent license agreement.

2.3 Recent Court Decisions in the U.K.

In addition to Germany, the U.K. has also attracted attention in recent years for the SEP lawsuits filed therein. Among them, the Unwired Planet v. Huawei case and the

Conversant v. Huawei/ZTE case are important in relation to the issues raised in this chapter.

In Unwired Planet v. Huawei, Unwired sued Huawei for Huawei's infringement of a SEP that Unwired Planet (hereinafter in this chapter "Unwired") had acquired from Ericsson. The district court accepted Unwired's claims and granted Unwired a global license. Huawei appealed to the UK Court of Appeal (England and Wales Court of Appeal), arguing that Unwired's claims for damages and injunction were in violation of the FRAND commitment and violated Article 102 of the TFEU. However, the UK Court of Appeal held that (1) it is inefficient to set out SEP licensing conditions on a country-by-country basis, and a global license is compatible with the FRAND commitment; (2) the "non-discriminatory" requirement does not mean that the SEP holder always need to the license on the same terms; (3) even if the licensor had decided to file a lawsuit without prior consultation with the other party, this would not immediately cause its conduct to violate Article 102 of the TFEU. Huawei thus appealed to the U.K. Supreme Court.

On the other hand, in Conversant v. Huawei/ZTE, Conversant sued Huawei and ZTE for alleged infringement of Conversant's patents, and, as a remedy, sought a FRAND licensing fee with respect to a license under the multinational patent portfolio. In response, Huawei and ZTE filed a complaint against Conversant in the U.K. Court of Appeals for the calculation of a license fee under the FRAND terms with respect to the multinational patent portfolio. They argued that Conversant's patents are invalid or not essential to the ETSI standard, that the U.K. accounts for only 1% and 0.07% of their worldwide sales, respectively, that this case is, in effect, an infringement of a foreign patent whose validity is in question, and that the English court does not have jurisdiction, or even if it does, the Chinese court would be more appropriate as a forum (venue) under the forum non conveniens doctrine. In response, the UK Court of Appeals held that there was no problem for the English court to hear and decide the case. Huawei and ZTE therefore appealed to the Supreme Court of the U.K.

The UK Supreme Court unanimously dismissed Huawei and ZTE's appeal in two cases and ruled that the UK courts have jurisdiction in cases regarding the licensing terms of a multinational patent portfolio for contractual arrangements under ETSI IPR policy, as follows ([2020] UKSC 37).

Specifically, first, concerning the jurisdictional question of whether the English courts can determine the global licensing terms of a multinational patent portfolio, the court held that, although issues concerning the validity and infringement of patents are determined by the courts of the country that granted the patents, the English courts can determine the global licensing terms, established on the basis of ETSI's patent policy, of a multinational patent portfolio that includes foreign patents.

Second, as to whether the Chinese courts would be a more appropriate forum for resolving this dispute than the English courts, Huawei and ZTE argued that the Chinese courts would be a more appropriate forum, but the UK Supreme Court held that unless all parties agreed that the Chinese courts have jurisdiction, the English courts have the necessary jurisdiction to determine the terms of the global FRAND license.

Third, regarding the interpretation of the "non-discrimination" requirement of the FRAND terms, the UK Supreme Court rejected Huawei and ZTE's argument that SEP holder is required to provide the same or similar terms to all licensees unless the SEP holder provides an objective reason for treating licensees differently, and held that the SEP holder is not required to grant licenses to all similarly situated licensees on terms equivalent to the most favorable license terms. Put differently, the Supreme Court ruled that a "general" rather than a "hard edge" nondiscrimination obligation would suffice.

Fourth, as to whether it is an abuse of a dominant market position and a violation of Article 102 TFEU when a SEP holder brings an injunction action without offering a license under FRAND terms, the UK Supreme Court held that it is generally accepted that bringing an injunction action without a warning or prior consultation with the alleged infringer may constitute a violation of Article 102 TFEU, but the nature of the warning or consultation depends on the circumstances and nature of the individual case, and the warning or consultation does not necessarily have to follow the procedure established by the CJEU preliminary ruling in the Huawei v. ZTE case.

Fifth, the UK Supreme Court rejected the argument that even if the implementer infringed the SEP, the court should only award damages in lieu of an injunction. This is because there is no risk that Unwired or Conversant will use the threat of an injunction as a means of charging exorbitant fees, since the SEP holder's FRAND offer, which is confirmed by the court, is a prerequisite for the exercise of Unwired's or Conversant's rights. In brief, the U.K. Supreme Court has also ruled in favor of SEP holders.

As a recent trend, both the U.K. and German courts have made the holdout of SEP implementers an issue, and seem to recognize that the patent holder could sue any implementer in a lawsuit as long as its patent is valid. The concept of "license to all" does not seem to be persuasive to the European courts. However, what constitute FRAND licensing terms and FRAND royalty rates are still in a puzzling situation, as the courts in Europe, the U.S., and Japan, as well as in China and South Korea, have very different views on this matter. Given this situation, it is difficult to establish uniform international rules at present time. However, the CJEU's preliminary ruling in the Huawei v. ZTE case indicated the possibility of "abuse of a dominant market position," and the UK Supreme Court and the German BGH both share the same point in that they leave open the possibility of violating Article 102 TFEU in their rulings. It is important to note that the application of competition law is the last resort. In Japan, the concept of "abuse of rights", as presented in the IP High Court's 2014 decision in Apple v. Samsung, is currently adopted, and in this respect, although the applicable laws and regulations differ from those in Europe and the United States, the underlying philosophies share common ground. The following section will discuss the three issues specified in Sect. 1 and give a tentative summary and critical analysis based on the abovementioned discussion.

3 Necessity of Rule Formation Concerning the Negotiation Process of SEP Licenses

3.1 Inter-industry Licensing in the Supply Chain

The case in which cross-industry licensing in the supply chain becomes an issue refers to a situation in which the SEP holder and the implementor have conflicting opinions as to whether the SEP holder who has made a FRAND commitment should be imposed with a "license to all" obligation or only an "access for all" obligation. To be specific, the SEP holder side argues that when the SEP holder requests the end-product manufacturer to join the license negotiation, it is inappropriate for the end-product mantufacturer not to respond to the negotiation while asserting that the counterparty of the negotiation should be the component manufacturer. The SEP holder side claimed that the concept of "license to all" should not be adopted, that the interpretation of the non-discrimination requirement should be only based on the "access for all" concept. On the other hand, the end-product manufacturer side argues that the SEP holder should adopt the "license to all" approach because it is discriminatory and contrary to FRAND obligations for the SEP holder to refuse to negotiate when the component manufacturer requests the SEP holder to join the license negotiation.

In Japan, the "license to all" concept seems to be adopted by the government. There is no precedent case regarding the "license to all" approach, but the Ministry of Economy, Trade and Industry (METI) (Manufacturing Industries Bureau), has expressed its opinion that the "license to all" approach is appropriate because of the following two reasons. First, in light of the fact that SEPs require "non-discrimination" as a FRAND condition, license negotiations should not be treated in a discriminatory manner depending on the transaction stage of potential implementers. Second, in the case of multi-component products, the negotiating entity should not be limited to the end-product manufacturer, because a component manufacturer with detailed knowledge of its component product on which the SEP is implemented may exist at any transaction stages in the supply chain. It would be more appropriate for the SEP holder to negotiate with these component manufacturers in order to calculate the proper license fee.

This issue ultimately boils down to the question of how the burden should be allocated within the supply chain. As mentioned at the beginning of this chapter, for example, in a scenario where the SEP holder denies the "license to all" concept, rejects license requests from the component manufacturer, and negotiates only with the end-product manufacturer, the end-product manufacturer may ask its upstream Tier 1 supplier to compensate for the license fee it paid to the SEP holder based on the patent indemnification clause included in the contract. The Tier 1 supplier may then try to request its upstream Tier 2 supplier to compensate for its payments but eventually fails to obtain compensation owing to its inferior negotiating position compared to the Tier 2 supplier. The problem is that the disparity in bargaining power prevents the Tier 1 supplier from doing so. In this case, the license fee is ultimately borne by the Tier 1 supplier, and the Tier 1 supplier may result in bankruptcy as a consequence. What constitutes fairness in the allocation of the burden within the supply chain is the fundamental question. The actual situation of patent indemnification varies greatly depending on the technology and the power balance among licensing and licensed companies. Patent indemnification is a business contractual issue, and it seems difficult to uniformly regulate it because it varies greatly depending on individual circumstances. For example, in the automobile industry, the basic concensus is that the supplier who researched, developed, and manufactured parts installed in automobiles should guarantee the safety of those parts to automobile manufacturers. In a similar thought, since the patent right is implemented by the component supplier that is responsible for its product, the component supplier should compensate the automobile manufacturers for the paid licensing fees. By contrast, in the semiconductor industry, it is common that semiconductor manufacturers claim that they do not take responsibility for patent infringement because thet simply manufacture and sell chips and they will not compensate for the patent infringement because they do not directly infringe. As described above, when it comes to IP compensation, the business practices differ greatly from industry to industry, and the opinions of the industry have not yet been consolidated, so it would be premature to establish guidelines to impose a certain level of discipline. An official guide titled "Guide to Licensing Negotiations involving Standard Essential Patents", published by the JPO, also only states both sides of the argument.

From the perspective of competition law, however, as long as a FRAND commitment has been made, the "non-discrimination" requirement should be applied regardless of the level of the supply chain, and it should be understood that a SEP holder with market dominance should not be allowed to unreasonably refuse a request for licensing of a SEP from Tier 1 or Tier 2 Supplier in the abovementioned example. The Joint Guidelines (CWA95000), published by the European Committee for Electrotechnical Standardization (CENELEC) and the European Committee for Standardization (CEN), the latter of which is the body responsible for standardization in areas other than electrical engineering (CENELEC) and telecommunications (ETSI), also states that "FRAND licenses should be made available to anyone wishing to implement the relevant standard. Denying licenses to some implementers is contrary to the promise of FRAND" (Core Principle 2), and it seems that this should be the premise of competition law thinking. The Guidelines for the Use of Intellectual Property under the Antimonopoly Act, published by the JFTC, also states that, "Refusal to license or bringing an action for injunction against a party who is willing to take a license by a FRAND-encumbered SEP holder, or refusal to license or bringing an action for injunction against a party who is willing to take a license by a FRAND-encumbered SEP holder after the withdrawal of the FRAND commitment for that SEP may fall under the exclusion of business activities of other entrepreneurs by making it difficult to research and develop, produce or sell the products adopting the standards." This interpretation should be applied even in the phase of selection of licensees, where "license to all" is an issue.

This issue is also concerned with the question of how to limit the SEP holder's right to seek an injunction on its SEPs. As ruled by the Japanese IP High Court in the Apple v. Samsung case, the exercise of the patent right to seek an injunction by a SEP holder who has made a FRAND commitment is not allowed because it constitutes abuse of rights (Article l, para. 3 of the Civil Code) when the other party succeeds in proving that the SEP holder has made a FRAND commitment and that the other party is willing to take the license on FRAND terms. However, the Japanese government seems to be circumspect about introducing a clarifying patent misuse provision that limits the exercise of the patent right to seek an injunction into the Patent Act, according to the discussions at the Industrial Structure Council of the METI.

On the other hand, in the U.S., the Department of Justice (DOJ)'s "Updated Response to Electrical and Electronics Engineers, Incorporated's 2015 Request for a Business Review Letter" (September, 2020) stated that the SEP holder has the right to seek an injunction against SEP implementers, and empasized the risk of holdout of SEP implementers rather than that of holdup of SEP holders, which was previously emphasized in the 2015 version "Response to Electrical and Electronics Engineers, Incorporated".

In any event, there is no dispute in Japan that the exercise of patent right to seek an injunction is limited within the scope of abuse of rights under the Civil Code, and that such exercise would also constitute abuse of rights if it is found to be in violation of the Antimonopoly Act. Thus, it is necessary to further examine court cases and analyze under what circumstances the exercise of the right to seek an injunction by the SEP holder constitutes a violation of the Antimonopoly Act.

3.2 Patent Pools and Their Evaluation

There are various types and forms of patent pools, as discussed in Sect. 1. It is impractical in terms of time and cost for various implementers to negotiate with all SEP holders in the world and conclude individual license agreements. In the first place, it is economically and socially desirable that SEPs are used by a large number of users. Therefore, ideally, it would be more efficient in terms of transaction costs if all SEP holders joined the same international patent pool and implementers concluded license agreements with the patent pool under reasonable terms and conditions, but this has not been the case in reality and is unlikely to happen. In addition, even if a group consisting of patent holders is called a patent pool, in reality, it may be a joint licensing organization for the purpose of charging exorbitant royalty fees. From the perspective of competition law, a monitoring system is thus essential to ensure that licensing conditions by patent pools are not unreasonable.

3.3 *Necessity of Information Provision Rules in License Negotiation Process*

Finally, we would like to hignlight the necessity of information provision rules in the license negotiation process. This has often been pointed out by government study groups. The Huawei v. ZTE decision, which functions as a precedent, laid out the measures to be taken by both the SEP holder and the implementer at each stage of license negotiation. The UK Supreme Court and the German BGH also examined the cases in accordance with the framework of the Huawei v. ZTE decision, as discussed in Sect. 2, but there is no uniformity in their decisions and conclusions. It appears that they made judgments in accordance with the case. On the other hand, there seems to be a trend worldwide, including Germany, to actively issue anti suit injunctions (injunctions against foreign lawsuits) in SEP litigation at the request of the parties. Although it is not clear whether such an order is possible in Japanese courts in the first place (in reality, it would be difficult), in order to reduce the risk of litigation that parties to SEP license agreements face in and outside of Japan, and from the perspective of dispute prevention, it is desirable to clarify the rules of the negotiation process on the premise that both parties have an obligation to negotiate in good faith during license negotiations.

Specifically, in the SEP license negotiation process, the SEP holder should present the patent number and specification for the relevant SEP, and a comparison table (the so-called claim chart) between the claims of the relevant SEP and the standard specifications covered by the relevant SEP, in order to identify the SEP to be negotiated. Then, both the SEP holder and the implementer should present the conditions that are considered to be FRAND together with the corresponding grounds. In this case, the essentiality determination system of SEPs, a service provided by the JPO, may also be of assistance in negotiations between the parties. In addition, when claiming infringement against an implementer, it may be required to specifically specify the mode of infringement while showing a claim chart. Also, it is common for the right holder to request the conclusion of a nondisclosure agreement (NDA) in the course of negotiations, and it appears that there is an underlying dissatisfaction on the part of the implementer that the right holder specifically requests an NDA even though there are no confidential matters involved. In order to prevent parties from falling into mutual distrust over the conclusion of an NDA, the right holder is required to present to the implementer the grounds on which the conclusion of an NDA is necessary, and similarly, the implementer is required to present to the right holder the grounds for refusing the conclusion of an NDA requested by the right holder.

Based on the formulation of the CJEU's ruling in the Huawei v. ZTE case, in the negotiation process of the SEP license, the starting point of the negotiation is that the implementer should express its intention, or the intention of the implementers involved in its supply chain, to conclude a contract under FRAND conditions with the SEP holder, on the premise that the SEP holder has made a FRAND commitment.

Then, the SEP holder is required to specify the license fee and the calculation method that it considers reasonable and to present the basis for such specification to such implementer. If the implementer refuses to conclude a contract under the license conditions presented, the licensee is required to present a counterproposal that includes the reason for the refusal and clear license conditions that it considers reasonable. This specific guidance on exchanging information, backed by the existence of the obligation of both parties to negotiate in good faith, may contribute to the reduction of SEP disputes.

In sum, it is important to visualize the rules with respect to the licensing of SEPs, which frequently results in disputes, based on the duty of good faith negotiation. Such rules, though based on the premise of private autonomy, may lead to the resolution of disputes between the parties. It is a global trend to adopt ex ante rules on information disclosure, etc. to supplement ex post competition law. In this regard, governments and courts naturally play a major role in shaping the direction of the rules.

4 Summary

In recent years, clashes over the licensing of SEPs have emerged in numerous countries around the world due to the proliferation of standards and the increased intricacy of the technologies necessary for such standards. Behind such litigations lies a system where SEP holders gather patent licensing fees from end-product manufacturers, as SEP holders can anticipate higher licensing fees by targeting end-product manufacturers to excercise their rights instead of negotiating with upstream suppliers of the end-product manufacturers. Nevertheless, industry has raised concerns that end-product manufacturers and component manufacturers will not obtain suitable compensation while licensing fees become more expensive, making it infeasible for them to do business. In response to this, the necessity of forming rules such as the exchanging of information between the parties has been emphasized from the viewpoint of resolving and preventing disputes between the parties. In light of such discussions, this chapter examines (1) the issue of how the burden of SEP licensing fess should be borne within the supply chain, (2) the evaluation of patent pool, and (3) the necessity of rules concerning the provision of information, etc. between the parties during the negotiation process, given the vast gap in claims between the parties regarding the license conditions and whom to negotiate with. The chapter first reviews recent major contentious cases in Europe, and examines some of the issues involved in each case.

When the inter-industry licensing in the supply chain becomes an issue, from the perspective of competition law, the "non-discrimination" requirement should be applied regardless of the level of the supply chain, as long as FRAND commitment has been made. The SEP holder with market dominance should not be allowed to unreasonably refuse the Tier 1 or Tier 2 suppliers's request to obtain the SEP's license. Second, in the assessment of patent pools, a monitoring system from the perspective of competition law is vital to ensure that license conditions are not unreasonable. Last, with regard to the need for information provision rules in the license negotiation process, a specific guidance may contribute to the reduction of SEP disputes, based on the existence of the obligation of both parties to negotiate in good faith. It is essential to visualize the rules with respect to the licensing of SEPs, which frequently results in disputes, based on the duty of good faith negotiation. Such rules, though based on the premise of private autonomy, may lead to the resolution of disputes between the parties.

References

CEN/CENELEC (2019) Core principles and approaches for licensing of standard essential patents. CWA 95000:2019: E
Department of Justice (2020a) Response to the Avanci LLC's request for a business review letter
Department of Justice (2020b) Updated response to electrical and electronics engineers, Incorporated's 2015 request for a business review letter
European Commission (2020) An intellectual property action plan to support the EU's recovery and resilience. COM(2020)760
Hayashi S (2016) CJEU Judgment on standard essential patent and competition law. EU Ho Kenkyu 1:3–23
Ito R (2021) New perspectives on intellectual property rights and competition policy in the United States and Europe. Fair Trade 847:18–27
Japan Fair Trade Commission (2005) Guidelines on standardization and patent pool arrangement
Japan Fair Trade Commission (2016 Revised) Guidelines for the use of intellectual property under the antimonopoly act
Japan Patent Office (2018a) Guide to licensing negotiations involving standard essential patents
Japan Patent Office (2018b) Manual of "Hantei" (advisory opinion) for essentiality check (revised version)
Matsunaga S (2021) Shift from the theory of restriction of SEP enforcements and the future issue. J Intellect Prop Assoc Jpn 17(3):5–14
Ministry of Economy, Trade and Industry (2020) Guide to fair value calculation of standard essential patents for multi-component products
Tanaka S, Hayashi S (2010) Revisiting the Pachinko patent pool case. J Soc Sci 61(2):135–162

Cases (In the Chronological Order of the Decisions)

Apple v. Samsung, IP High Court, Special Division (May 16, 2014), Case No. 2013 (Ne) 10043
Huawei v ZTE, Court of Justice (July 16 2015), Case No. C-170/13, EU:C:2015:477
Sisvel v. Haier, Regional Court of Düsseldorf (November 3, 2015), docket No. 4a O 93/14
Sisvel v. Haier, Higher Regional Court of Düsseldorf (March 30, 2017), docket No. I-15 U 66/15
Unwired Planet v Huawei, UK High Court of Justice (April 5, 2017), Case No. [2017] EWHC 711 (Pat)
Unwired Planet v Huawei, UK Court of Appeal (October 23, 2018), Case No. [2018] EWCA Civ 2344
Conversant v. Huawei and ZTE, UK Court of Appeal (January 30, 2019), Case No. [2019] EWCA Civ 38
Unwired Planet v. Huawei, Higher Regional Court of Düsseldorf (March 22, 2019), docket No. I-2 U 31/16
Philips v. Wiko, Higher Regional Court of Karlsruhe (October 30, 2019), docket No. 6 U 183/16
Sisvel v. Haier, Federal Court of Justice (May 5, 2020), docket No. KZR 36/17

Nokia v. Daimler, District Court of Mannheim (August 18, 2020), docket No. 2 O 34/19
Unwired Planet v. Huawei & Conversant v. Huawei and ZTE, UK Supreme Court (August 26, 2020), Case No. [2020] UKSC 37
Sharp v. Daimler, District Court of Munich (September 10, 2020), docket No. 7 O 8818/19
Sisvel v. Haier, Federal Court of Justice (November 24, 2020), docket No. KZR 35/17
Nokia v. Daimler, Regional Court of Düsseldorf (November 26,2020), docket No. 4c O 17/19

Chapter 11
Digital Society and Regulations: A Competition Policy Perspective

1 Introduction

In late December 2021, the Japanese government outlined the so-called "Five Digital Principles" and announced "Priority Plan for the Realization of a Digital Society". In the plan, the integrated reform of digital regulation and administration based on the digital principles is advocated, and it is expected that discussions toward legislation based on these principles or policies will accelerate in the near future. In view of this, this chapter considers the challenges and risks associated with the digitalization of society under these circumstances, as well as the state of law in digital society.

First, we would like to discuss the formation of the so-called "RegTech" (Regulation × Digital Technology) and its relevant issues in the era of Society 5.0. The image of the society in the context of Society 5.0 shows a different picture from that depicted in the first and second generations of digitalization. The first generation refers to the era of localized digitalization, in which the analog society is digitialized. In that era, the digitalization of the information, communications and telecommunications (ICT) industry was the main focus, and other industries were only promoting the digitalization of their own businesses by utilizing their own data as a tool to improve efficiency, so to speak.

In contrast, the developments in recent years are of the second generation. In other words, the digitalization proceeds not only in the ICT field but also in the entire industrial sector. Recent digital policies on the data-driven society is recognized as refering to this. In this second generation, the entire industrial structure will be digitialized, and a variety of services will be developed by fusing and linking data and information from both the physical and cyber spaces. This kind of Cyber Physical System (CPS) is considered to be the basic concept of this generation.

Regarding the CPS, reports of the Study Group on New Governance Models in Society 5.0 ("Government Innovation—Redesigning Law and Architecture for the Realization of Society 5.0" [July 13, 2020], and "Government Innovation—Toward the Design and Implementation of Agile Governance" [July 30, 2021]) have pointed out the following social changes resulting from the realization of Society 5.0, which

S. Hayashi and K. Arai, *Digitalization and Competition Policy in Japan*,
https://doi.org/10.1007/978-981-99-5310-3_11

is characterized by the CPS. That is, digital technology will become an indispensable foundation for daily life, and the object of trust will change from tangible objects to intangible ones (data and algorithms). The data that can be obtained will become large-scale and extensive.

Also, the influence of AI on the decision making process is likely to emerge. In addition, the state of the AI system is not not static but variable, which makes it difficult to predict the results and to control the variables, and in some cases, it may be challenging to identify the responsible entity. Furthermore, market dominance will be concentrated in the hands of the so-called "BigTech" companies, which are expanding globally. In light of these changes, the traditional model of governance, which is to create ex ante rules and make people comply with them, is likely to be dysfunctional in the Society 5.0 era. In view of this, the direction of "agile governance" or "from rule-based to goal-based legal regulations" is proposed in the reports. In other words, in order to realize Society 5.0, it is necessary to continuously monitor the various governance systems, such as corporations, laws and regulations, infrastructure, markets, and social norms, with the following considerations: (1) environmental and risk analysis, (2) goal setting, (3) system design, (4) real data, rather than governance with fixed rules and procedures in advance, (5) evaluation and improvement of the governance system to assess whether the initially set goals are achieved or not, and (6) the cycle of the agile governance model, which continuously analyzes whether the goals need to be adapted due to changes in the environment or risk conditions in which the governance system is embedded, should be continuously and rapidly rotated by multi-stakeholders.

However, the suitability of the agile governance model for the CPS is controversial. In other words, the question arises whether the risks to the society on which the CPS is based are not fully grasped because the functions of the digital platform have not been sufficiently analyzed in the structural analysis of the CPS. In addition, business operators seem to play a main role in the system of the agile governance, but they are basically entities aiming to pursue their own profits. The current CPS is mainly deployed in an ecosystem formed on the basis of digital platforms. Therefore, there is possibility that individual consumers and users be subjected to unfair treatment on such platforms. There are concerns about whether the current legal system is sufficient to remedy such individual infringements of consumer interests when they occur.

In addition, there are also concerns that the goal-based regulation may result in weakening the enforcement of laws and regulations from the viewpoint of assuring redress of victims, unless the goal is clearly defined and the failure to comply with the goal is subject to to the pursuit of responsibility.

The issues pointed out in the reports are understandable, but we feel that the approach to tackling these issues in these reports is somehow similar to that adopted in the software design or system engineering such as the standardization process of quality, performance or safety. However, the goal of performance or safety standards is relatively clear. Also, in the context of software design, it is quite understandable to use an agile approach in assembling a system when it is difficult to build the system with existing items. For example, OS and software are frequently updated. Without an agile approach, it would not be possible to commercialize a product in a limited period of time. How well such system engineering and software design concepts fit into the philosophy of social science, especially in terms of laws and regulations, is an issue to be addressed.

2 Regulations and Institutions Corresponding to Digitalization

As the process of protecting the public interest is becoming increasingly complicated and multifaceted, the issue of legitimacy of regulations requires a review of both inputs and outputs. With regard to this legitimacy, it should be considered to be in a relative relationship between the public and private sectors rather than in a dichotomy between them. Based on this thought, the content and evaluation of the Japanese government's proposal for the review of regulations and systems, especially the "Five Digital Principles" announced at the end of December 2021,will be discussed in this section The five digital principles are "digital completion and automation" and "agile governance," as well as "public–private partnership," "interoperability," and "common infrastructure use".

Although all of them seem desirable, some doubts remain when they are analyzed individually. It is good that digital completion is advancing, but, for example, it may be questionable whether the process of notarization, in which the client's intentions are fully confirmed during the process of meeting directly with a notary public and having such a specialist authenticate the document, can really be completed in a digital manner. In other words, there is a concern that the digital completion and automation may make a sham of the principle of will. Also, the principle of agile governance calls for the elimination of uniform qualification-based criteria, such as academic background and work experience as qualification requirements of a system, and promotes the substitution of technical skills and digital literacy for these criteria. However, its feasibility seems doubtful in reality.

In addition, the public–private partnership calls for the introduction of more joint regulation and self-regulation as a form of multi-stakeholder governance. Although there is a strong opinion that the so-called "soft law" is expected for digital platform regulations, the "soft law" cannot function properly unless it is accompanied with a hard law and enforcement mechanisms. Soft law without enforcement may become a dead letter. At present, there are many areas where enforcement needs to be further strengthened by either administrative or criminal penalties. Self-regulations that are completely voluntary and independent of the state and the market is rather an exception than the norm, and in the majority of cases self-regulations function at the request of the state, legal system, or pressure from the market. In this sense, the distinction between the self-regulation and joint regulation seems to be relative.

Regarding interoperability, one of the main topics that are discussed in the context of competition law and business law is how to avoid the lock-in by simplifying the system through API disclosure, obligations to open up APIs, etc. It is also important to ensure the equal-footing between domestic and foreign business operators through effective extraterritorial application. However, innovation may be hindered if excessive regulations apply to business operators. Rather, it seems that the focus of discussion should be the international standardization of regulations.

3 Joint Regulation

It should be noted that, in Japan, unlike the EU, the discussion on joint regulation may result in an unique one due to the common thought of public–private community. Some have pointed out the importance of being aware of the increased welfare of each citizen. For example, with regard to COCOA, a smartphone application that allows users to receive notifications about the possibility of contact with a person infected with COVID-19, it has a great social benefit in that the more users use the application, the more data the users provide, and the more efficient COCOA becomes. However, contact verification applications can only work if COVID-19-positive persons voluntarily register themselves as being positive. Therefore, the main benefit is altruistic: others who may have come into contact with the COVID-19-positive person would receive a notification and receive support from the public health center, such as a medical examination, as soon as possible. Although the social benefit expected from the increase in the number of registered users is exponential, the individual benefit enjoyed by each app user is relatively small. Thus, it is difficult to promote the installment of COCOA and expand the use of apps depending on the individual app user's sense of public duty. On the other hand, it can be positvely evaluated that the difficulty was overcome and the implementation of the COCOA project proceeded smoothly thanks to the cooperation of a large number of app users.

4 Discussion Regarding the Public

From the perspective of the "public," the idea of community, which carries the notion that every citizen should be aware of the increased total social welfare, is a very important issue. The public interest could not be realized just because of the introduction of joint regulation. Also, the rulemaking process should not be completely left to the private sector, nor should we take advantage of the joint regulation and in the end obscure where the responsibility lies.

The public and private interests are not dichotomous. It is possible to discuss them in a quasi-public manner. Such discussion focuses on the collective interests. It is necessary to construct incentive designs that take such collective interests into consideration. In doing so, there might be an issue as to how to coordinate and harmonize the measures for functional regulation, the design of rules for that purpose, and traditional sector-specific regulations. In this context, the creation of rules to establish a sustainable system, in which the stakeholders involved are satisfied in a way that is different from the aspects of predictability, maintenance of order, and law enforcement, must be emphasized. On top of that, it is important to examine the legislative facts. We can position the creation of rules as a process of verifying these facts, drawing up necessary social and legal rules while delivering messages to society as necessary, and finally having the court verify these rules.

In considering the legal design in the digital society, it is necessary to always consider the message for the future of new technology and law. In shaping the basic legal infrastructure of the digital society, it is believed that practitioners and researchers need to play a more collaborative and creative role in an interdisciplinary manner.

5 Competition Policy

In discussing the regulatory framework for the digital society, the role of competition policy must also be constantly examined. Among other things, it is necessary not only to offer recommendations from the perspective of competition policy, but also to actively enforce competition law in practice. It can be seen that competition law cases are becoming increasingly complex and complicated. Yet there have been relatively few competition law enforcement cases recently. More aggressive enforcement of competition law is desirable.

In addition, in light of the recent world situation, it is urgent to keep a close watch on cartel-like price hikes in the economy with inflationary tendencies. During deflationary periods, it is necessary to pay attention to price hikes through joint actions, but with ongoing inflaction continuing to rise, it is easier to raise prices through coordination under the pretext of raw material price hikes, etc. This is why there is a greater need for countermeasures, prevention, and incident management.

In addition, the third-generation evolution of generative AI has been remarkable today, especially from the latter half of 2022 onward. The use of AI for image processing, language processing, etc. will continue progressing, and we are seeing a substantial shift in the process of work as well as in the society. In such an environment, it will be necessary to seriously consider how to appropriately use and utilize AI for fact-finding and decision-making based on value as human activities.

6 Summary

With regard to the realization of digital society, there has been a call for an integrated reform of digital rules and public administration based on digital principles, and it is highly expected that progress towards legislation will accelerate based on these principles or policies. This chapter examines the issues and risks associated with the digitalization of society, as well as the legal state of a digital society. Concerning the issues of "RegTech", it is expected that data in the cyber-physical system (CPS) context will become large-scale and extensive in the form of Big Data, and that AI and other entities may become the primary decision-makers. Moreover, there is a risk of market dominance by the firms typified by the so-called "BigTech". In the discussion of regulations and systems in the digital era, the question of the legitimacy of regulations arises as the process of achieving public interest varies, and further research and examination on the voluntary regulation is also necessary. Additionally, it is important that citizens are aware of the fact that joint regulation advances the welfare of individual citizens. As to the discussion on the "public", it is essential to clarify where responsibility lies, as well as to coordinate and harmonize the rules with traditional sector-specific regulations. As for the role of competition policy, it is imperative to increase the number of law enforcement cases, to monitor cartel-like price hikes in an inflationary world, and to seriously consider how to properly utilize AI in fact-finding and value judgment, which have been done by humans, in the evolution of generative AI.

Correction to: Digitalization and Competition Policy in Japan

Correction to:
S. Hayashi and K. Arai, *Digitalization and Competition Policy in Japan*, https://doi.org/10.1007/978-981-99-5310-3

In the original version of the book belated update has been done. In the chapters 2 and 10 few references were added in the reference section. The correction chapters and the book have been updated with the changes.

The updated version of these chapters can be found at
https://doi.org/10.1007/978-981-99-5310-3_2,
https://doi.org/10.1007/978-981-99-5310-3_10

S. Hayashi and K. Arai, *Digitalization and Competition Policy in Japan*,
https://doi.org/10.1007/978-981-99-5310-3_12

Final Words

We extend our sincere appreciation for the invaluable time you dedicated to scrutinizing our collaborative work "Digitalization and Competition Policy in Japan". During the writing process of this book, there were various challenges, but we overcame them with unwavering fortitude and diligence.

The temporary departure of one of the authors, Shuya Hayashi, on a year-long research expedition to Germany presented the first challenge. Nevertheless, our unwavering dedication to this project enabled us to triumph over all impediments and bring it to fruition. Overcoming communication obstacles that arose due to our physical distance, we relied on digital mediums including email and online conferencing systems.

The second challenge we encountered was the arduous task of exploring competition law in the digital age, particularly within the current context that requires familiarity with regulations governing digital spaces, such as information law. Despite the need for considerable effort and intellectual acumen, we are confident that our collective expertise would enable us to offer a fresh perspective to readers.

Furthermore, we encountered the third challenge in the digital realm, such as utilizing digital means during the COVID-19 pandemic for the practice of competition law and the application of economic theories in antitrust matters, including criminal cartel cases in the United States. Moreover, the advent of generative AI posed another significant challenge, and we faced mounting pressure to deliver genuine added value.

Notwithstanding all these obstacles, we persevered and were able to complete this book. We would like to extend our gratitude to all those involved.

S. Hayashi and K. Arai, *Digitalization and Competition Policy in Japan*,
https://doi.org/10.1007/978-981-99-5310-3

MIX
Papier aus verantwortungsvollen Quellen
Paper from responsible sources
FSC® C105338
FSC
www.fsc.org

If you have any concerns about our products,
you can contact us on
ProductSafety@springernature.com

In case Publisher is established outside the EU,
the EU authorized representative is:
Springer Nature Customer Service Center GmbH
Europaplatz 3, 69115 Heidelberg, Germany

Printed by Libri Plureos GmbH
in Hamburg, Germany